MARCIA L. TATE

CORWIN PRESS
Classroom

For information:

Corwin Press
A SAGE Company
2455 Teller Road
Thousand Oaks, California 91320
CorwinPress.com

SAGE, Ltd.
1 Oliver's Yard
55 City Road
London EC1Y 1SP
United Kingdom

SAGE India Pvt. Ltd.
B 1/I 1 Mohan Cooperative
Industrial Area
Mathura Road, New Delhi
India 110 044

SAGE Asia-Pacific Pvt. Ltd.
33 Pekin Street #02-01
Far East Square
Singapore 048763

ISBN: 978-1-4129-5952-0

This book is printed on acid-free paper.

08   09   10   11   12   10 9 8 7 6 5 4 3 2 1

Executive Editor: Kathleen Hex
Managing Developmental Editor: Christine Hood
Editorial Assistant: Anne O'Dell
Developmental Writers: Q. L. Pearce and Gina Capaldi
Developmental Editor: Heera Kang
Proofreader: Carrie Reiling
Art Director: Anthony D. Paular
Design Project Manager: Jeffrey Stith
Cover Designers: Monique Hahn and Lisa Miller
Illustrator: Jane Yamada
Cover Illustrator: Corbin Hillam
Design Consultant: The Development Source

GRADES 6–8
SOCIAL STUDIES

TABLE OF CONTENTS

Connections to Standards

This chart shows the national social studies standards covered in each chapter.

SOCIAL STUDIES	Standards are covered on pages
Understand culture and cultural diversity.	41, 46, 54, 62, 91
Understand the ways human beings view themselves in and over time.	8, 29, 46, 54, 62
Understand the interactions among people, places, and environments.	8, 12, 17, 29, 33, 54, 62, 66
Understand individual development and identity.	29, 33, 35, 41, 46, 54, 62, 66, 70, 91
Understand interactions among individuals, groups, and institutions.	8, 17, 24, 29, 33, 35, 59, 62, 70, 74, 78, 88, 91
Understand how people create and change structures of power, authority, and governance.	8, 35, 59, 70, 78, 81, 88, 91
Understand how people organize for the production, distribution, and consumption of goods and services.	18, 78, 84
Understand relationships among science, technology, and society.	24, 74, 84, 88
Understand global connections and interdependence.	12, 74, 78, 84
Understand the ideals, principles, and practices of citizenship in a democratic republic.	35, 59, 81, 84

Introduction

Think back to your years as a student. Which classes do you remember the most? Many of us fondly remember those dynamic classes that engaged our attention. However, we can just as easily remember those classes in which lectures seemed to last forever. The difference is that we can usually recall something we *learned* in the dynamic classroom. This is because our brains were engaged.

The latest in brain research reiterates what good teachers already know—student engagement is crucial to learning. Using various technological methods, scientists have found that the use of games to energize and engross students is one of the best strategies to activate learning. Can students truly learn content while playing games? Walk by a classroom where students are playing a game, and you might see chaos at first glance. Look again—this is actually collaboration. Amidst the buzz of competition, students are willingly discussing material once considered bland. When students "play," they interact using all of their senses, stimulating brain function that helps retain content.

How to Use This Book

Correlated with the national standards for social studies, this book provides games that will engage all students, even reluctant learners. The games review concepts in geography and maps, American history, world history, world cultures, and government and citizenship. They follow a format that promotes learning and retention, including introduction, focus activity, modeling, guided practice, check for understanding, closing, and independent practice. Using these strategies ensures that students are active participants in their own learning, not passive bystanders.

Students will build geography and map-reading skills, understand how physical and social environments affect a region, learn how important individuals and events shaped history, recognize different historical viewpoints, study the roles of government and citizenship, and more!

Games can be fun, lively, and spirited. The little bit of extra effort it takes to implement games into your curriculum will reap loads in student involvement. You can expect high emotion, healthy rivalry, and exhilarating debate. Thus, set firm ground rules when starting any classroom game. Prepare prizes at your discretion, but typically the spirit of competition and sense of accomplishment are enough to fuel a lively game. Watch as once disinterested students transform before your eyes. Just like the fond memories you keep of that dynamic class years ago, your students will remember the fun they had in your class and, more important, what they learned.

Put It Into Practice

Lecture and repetitive worksheets have long been the traditional method of delivering knowledge and reinforcing learning. While some higher-achieving students may engage in this type of learning, educators now know that actively engaging students' brains is not a luxury, but a necessity if students are truly to acquire and retain content, not only for tests but for life.

The 1990s were dubbed the Decade of the Brain because millions of dollars were spent on brain research. Educators today should know more about how students learn than ever before. Learning styles theories that call for student engagement have been proposed for decades, as evidenced by research such as Howard Gardner's theory of multiple intelligences (1983), Bernice McCarthy's 4MAT Model (1990), and VAKT (visual, auditory, kinesthetic, tactile) learning styles theories.

I have identified 20 strategies that, according to brain research and learning styles theories, appear to correlate with the way the brain learns best. I have observed hundreds of teachers—regular education, special education, and gifted. Regardless of the classification or grade level of the students, exemplary teachers consistently use these 20 strategies to deliver memorable classroom instruction and help their students understand and retain vast amounts of content.

These 20 brain-based instructional strategies include the following:

1. Brainstorming and Discussion

2. Drawing and Artwork

3. Field Trips

4. Games

5. Graphic Organizers, Semantic Maps, and Word Webs

6. Humor

7. Manipulatives, Experiments, Labs, and Models

8. Metaphors, Analogies, and Similes

9. Mnemonic Devices

10. Movement

11. Music, Rhythm, Rhyme, and Rap

12. Project-based and Problem-based Instruction

13. Reciprocal Teaching and Cooperative Learning

14. Role Play, Drama, Pantomime, Charades

15. Storytelling

16. Technology

17. Visualization and Guided Imagery

18. Visuals

19. Work Study and Apprenticeships

20. Writing and Journals

This book features Instructional Strategy 4: Games. While playing games, students use teamwork, interpersonal skills, and movement, and experience the spirit of competition. They actively express emotions, interact with friends, and explore new challenges of learning with immediate feedback and success (Beyers, 1998). The inherent joy of play is the brain's link from a world of reality to the development of creativity. In addition, play speeds up the brain's maturation process with built-in elements of competition, novelty, acknowledgement, and time limitations (Jensen, 2001).

Games involve active learning. The games in this book help students learn on a variety of levels. Some games involve quiet concentration, some energized, kinesthetic movement. However, all of the games involve interpersonal skills of sharing, discussing, creating, and working effectively with a team or a partner. Once students are familiar with how a game is constructed, they can use these same ideas to create their own versions of the game. Brain research shows that when students are involved in the design and construction of a learning game, the game's effectiveness is enhanced (Wolfe, 2001).

Students are no strangers to competition. They face it regularly—vying for chair placement in orchestra, playing team sports, or auditioning for the school play. That same sense of competition and teamwork can take place in the classroom. Board games, card games, memory games, trivia games, games that encourage physicality, games that involve using the senses, and games that involve creative imagination all provide the social stimulation, discussion, movement, and creativity that make students actively participate in learning.

These memorable strategies help students make sense of learning by focusing on the ways the brain learns best. Fully supported by the latest brain research, the games presented in this resource provide the tools you need to boost motivation, energy, and most important, the academic achievement of your students.

CHAPTER 1

Geography and Maps

Lewis and Clark's Living Timeline

Objective

Students will study the timeframe, conflicts, and results of the Lewis and Clark expedition.

Small-group projects reinforce classroom learning. This game promotes collaboration and problem solving skills. Student groups will scavenge for materials to construct a "living" timeline of Lewis and Clark's search for the Northwest Passage.

Materials

- Expedition Entries reproducibles
- scissors
- dry-erase marker
- masking tape
- United States wall map, laminated
- voting box (e.g., shoe box)
- reference materials about Lewis and Clark

1. Ask students if they have ever been on a scavenger hunt. Tell them they will go on a scavenger hunt to learn more about Lewis and Clark's expedition.

2. Introduce the idea that since the birth of the nation, passage by water was an essential means of transportation. Our young country was rapidly building canals and opening up waterways. There were no steam engines, railroads, or cars. People traveled mostly by ship, horse, and carriage.

3. Explain that on January 18, 1803, President Thomas Jefferson requested money from Congress for an expedition to find the Northwest Passage, a water route from the Missouri River to the Pacific. Ask for reasons why Jefferson might have pushed for the expedition. Suggest that because he was a scientist, he was curious about unknown plants, animals, and people that lived beyond the Missouri.

Part 1: Mark the Trail

1. Photocopy the **Expedition Entries reproducibles (pages 10–11)** and cut out the cards. Give a card to each student. (If there are more students than cards, let some students pair up to work together.) Provide a laminated wall map of the United States. Using a dry-erase marker, draw Lewis and Clark's expedition route on the map.

2. Invite students to tape the entries on the map in chronological order. Model the first entry by taping it to the beginning of the route. Students must tape their entries in the correct order by date.

Part 2: Learn What Happened

1. For the next part of the game, tell students they will make a journal of information about the travels of Lewis and Clark and the Corps of Discovery. Divide the class into teams of five and have each team choose a location on the timeline. Explain that teams will research these five topics about the area:
   - plants and animals
   - native people
   - weather
   - land features
   - what happened to the Corps of Discovery at that location

2. Suggest that each team think of a team name. Each team member then researches one of the topics and writes a one-paragraph journal entry. Have them write as if they were part of the Corps. Ask teams to make a creative cover and staple the journal pages together.

Part 3: Make the Living Timeline

1. Direct students to compile a scavenger hunt list of props to gather for the living history timeline. The list should include items from their journal research. Items might include articles brought from home, crafts, plants, or sketches and drawings. Allow time for teams to collect the items.

2. Prepare the base of the living timeline. Make a trail of masking tape on the floor that weaves around the classroom. Mark the start and finish points and set up a voting box at the end.

3. Have each team review the wall map. Then, similar to a museum exhibit, have them set up their journals and scavenged items in the proper order on the tape timeline. Now they have created a living timeline!

4. Encourage students to pretend they are visiting a museum. They can look at the props, read the journals, and vote for the best display. The team with the most votes wins.

5. Afterward, discuss some of the most successful elements of each display.

Expedition Entries

Summer 1803: Lewis oversees construction of the keelboat; he chooses William Clark and the rest of the Corps as he travels down the Ohio River.

September 25, 1804: The Corps has a tense encounter with the Teton Sioux.

Fall/Winter 1803: The Corps camps for the winter along the Ohio River.

October 24, 1804: The Corps arrives at the villages of the Mandan and Hidatsa.

May 14, 1804: The Corps of Discovery begins the journey up the Missouri River.

November 4, 1804: Lewis and Clark hire interpreters, the French-Canadian fur trader, Toussaint Charbonneau, and his American Indian wife, Sacagawea.

August 3, 1804: The Corps holds a council with Oto and Missouri Indians.

April 29, 1805: First grizzly bear killed near the Yellowstone River in Montana. Boats nearly overturn with Sacagawea saving the most important possessions.

August 20, 1804: Sergeant Charles Floyd dies of natural causes.

May 31, 1805: The Corps reaches the White Cliffs region. Later, they reach an unknown fork of the Missouri.

August 30, 1804: The Corps holds a council with the Yankton Sioux.

June 13, 1805: Men must carry all their gear, including the canoes, because of massive water cascades.

Early September 1804: The Corps enters the Great Plains.

July 1805: The expedition reaches the Three Forks of the Missouri River.

Expedition Entries

August 12, 1805: Lewis finds the headwaters of the Missouri River and crosses the Continental Divide and Lemhi Pass. The Corps acknowledges that there is no Northwest Passage.

October 16, 1805: The expedition reaches the Columbia River.

August 17, 1805: The main party arrives at the Shoshone camp. Sacagawea recognizes her long-lost brother, who is a Shoshone chief.

Late October 1805: The Corps runs their canoes through treacherous rapids.

September 9, 1805: The men camp near Traveler's Rest and prepare for the mountain crossings.

November 7, 1805: Clark believes he has found the Pacific Ocean. The location is actually the widened estuary of the Columbia River.

September 11, 1805: The Corps ascends the steep Bitterroot Range (Rocky Mountains). The walk is more than 160 miles.

November 24, 1805: The Corps finally reaches the Pacific Ocean. First democratic vote taken by entire Corps, including Sacagawea and Clark's slave, York.

September 23, 1805: Starving Corps members emerge from the mountains to the villages of the Nez Perce Indians.

March 23, 1806: The Corps prepares to head for home after a long, rainy winter. Fort handed over to Clatsop Indians.

October 7, 1805: The Corps pushes off down Clearwater River with new dugout canoes. They use techniques learned from the Nez Perce.

September 23, 1806: The Corps reaches St. Louis nearly two and one-half years after their journey began.

Geography Quiz Kids

Materials

- Geography Quiz Kids Game Cards reproducibles
- map and globe
- poster board
- letter envelopes
- scissors
- tape or glue
- colored markers
- index cards
- noisemakers or bells
- stopwatch

Objective

Students will play a game to review geometry terminology, including land features and maps and globes.

Learning geographical concepts is critical in order for students to understand the world around them. This requires students to learn many new terms and definitions. This game is played similarly to the popular game show *Jeopardy®* (a registered trademark of Jeopardy Productions, Inc. dba Merv Griffin Enterprises Corporation), but teaches essential geographical vocabulary and concepts.

1. Ahead of time, make a Geography Quiz Kids board using letter-sized envelopes cut in half to create pockets and attaching those pockets in a 4 x 5 array on poster board. Write the column headers *Land Features*, *Maps and Globes*, *Places*, and *General Geography*, and label each column of pockets *100*, *200*, *300*, *400*, and *500* (point values) from top to bottom.

2. Photocopy the **Geography Quiz Kids Game Cards reproducibles (pages 14–16)** and cut out the boxes. Glue each box to a separate index card to make game cards. Place the cards into the game board pockets by level of difficulty. Also include two "Double Bonus" cards hidden behind two of the game cards, making them worth double points.

3. Warm up students for the game by showing them a map and a globe. Explain that these tools were developed to help people better understand their world. Point out climactic regions, waterways, and mountains. Point out the components of a map, such as longitude and latitude lines. Review vocabulary and concepts from earlier geography lessons.

4. Tell students they will play a game based on the popular game show *Jeopardy®*. Just like the game show, students will be given an answer, and they must respond with a question. If they do not respond with a question, they will lose their turn. For example:

   Clue: *Land with water surrounding it on all sides.*

   Student Answer: *What is an island?*

5. To play the game, divide the class into teams and give each team a noisemaker or bell to "buzz in" with the correct answer. Choose a team to go first and have that team choose a question from the game board by category and point value (e.g., *Places for 300*).

978-1-4129-5952-0

Practice with a few game cards and allow each team to play one practice round.

6. Read the answer aloud. The first team to buzz in gets first chance to respond. If they respond correctly, they win that number of points and choose the next card. If they answer incorrectly, or take longer than five seconds to respond, they lose that number of points from their score, and the other teams get a chance to buzz in with the correct response.

7. Before you begin playing a real game, make sure students understand how to identify the game cards and point values. Remind them that they must respond with questions, not answers. If they do not, they lose a turn.

8. Have a scorekeeper from each team keep track of his or her team's score on the board, including negative totals if the team loses more points than earned. The team with the most points at the end of the game wins!

Extended Learning

Include a second set of more difficult questions and answers for a final Geography Quiz Kids question. Before the final card is read, teams must decide how many points to wager (how much of their total points). This will determine the final winner.

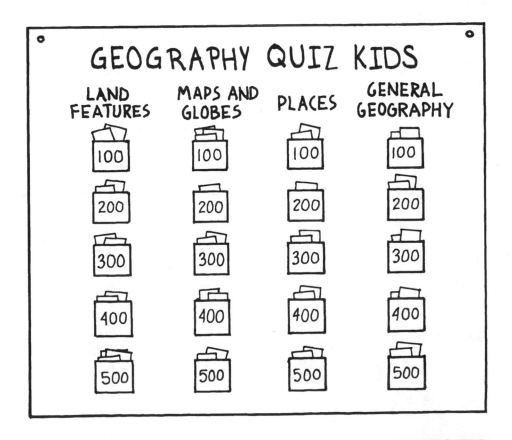

Geography Quiz Kids Game Cards

Land Features
Clue: A natural formation of fresh water that runs into a larger body of water
Answer: *What is a river?*

Land Features
Clue: A very deep valley
Answer: *What is a canyon?*

Land Features
Clue: Land with water surrounding it on all sides
Answer: *What is an island?*

Land Features
Clue: Body of water with land surrounding it on all sides
Answer: *What is a lake?*

Land Features
Clue: Highest kind of land formed by the earth pushing upward
Answer: *What are mountains?*

Land Features
Clue: Large, low, flat region of land
Answer: *What is a plain?*

Land Features
Clue: Low land between hills or mountains, often carved by glaciers
Answer: *What is a valley?*

Land Features
Clue: Land formed at a river's mouth, made from deposits carried downstream
Answer: *What is a delta?*

Land Features
Clue: Large body of ice that moves down a mountain, eroding soil and forming a huge valley
Answer: *What is a glacier?*

Land Features
Clue: Narrow strip of land with water on three sides
Answer: *What is a peninsula?*

Land Features
Clue: Land that is high and fairly flat
Answer: *What is a plateau?*

Maps and Globes
Clue: One of the main directions on a compass: north, south, east, west
Answer: *What is a cardinal direction?*

Maps and Globes
Clue: Diagram on a map that shows compass directions
Answer: *What is a compass rose?*

Land Features
Clue: Narrow strip of land connecting two larger areas, with water on both sides
Answer: *What is an isthmus?*

Maps and Globes
Clue: It is 0° latitude, dividing Earth's north and south hemispheres
Answer: *What is the equator?*
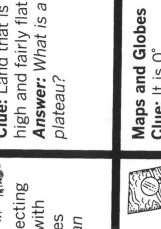

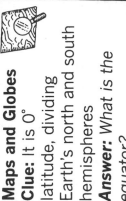

Maps and Globes
Clue: Unit of measurement equal to 1/360 of a circle
Answer: *What is a degree?*

Geography Quiz Kids Game Cards

Maps and Globes
Clue: Imaginary line joining points on Earth, equal distance north and south of the equator
Answer: *What is latitude?*

Maps and Globes
Clue: Line on a map that runs east to west, used to measure latitude
Answer: *What is a parallel?*

Places
Clue: Name for a mountain system in south-central Europe
Answer: *What are the Alps?*

Places
Clue: Biome characterized by low rainfall and little or no vegetation
Answer: *What is desert?*

Maps and Globes
Clue: Imaginary line that measures distance east or west of the Prime Meridian
Answer: *What is longitude?*

Maps and Globes
Clue: It is 0° longitude, the line from which longitude is calculated
Answer: *What is the Prime Meridian?*

Places
Clue: Earth's longest mountain range, found underneath the ocean
Answer: *What is the Mid-Atlantic Range?*

Places
Clue: Biome with grasses and low-lying plants
Answer: *What is grassland?*

Maps and Globes
Clue: Line on a map that runs north to south, used to measure longitude
Answer: *What is a meridian?*

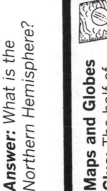

Maps and Globes
Clue: Map showing the size/shape of land and water; distortions located only at the edges
Answer: *What is a Robinson projection?*

Places
Clue: The world's highest mountain peak
Answer: *What is Mount Everest?*

Places
Clue: Biome made of freshwater and marine environments
Answer: *What is aquatic?*

Maps and Globes
Clue: The half of Earth north of the equator
Answer: *What is the Northern Hemisphere?*

Maps and Globes
Clue: The half of Earth south of the equator
Answer: *What is the Southern Hemisphere?*

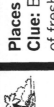

Places
Clue: The world's largest volcano
Answer: *What is Manua Loa?*

Places
Clue: Coldest biome of treeless plains, between the ice cap and the timberline
Answer: *What is tundra?*

Geography Quiz Kids Game Cards

Places
Clue: The world's largest island and smallest continent
Answer: *What is Australia?*

General Geography
Clue: Current of warm water from the Gulf of Mexico to Newfoundland
Answer: *What is the Gulf Stream?*

General Geography
Clue: Fracture in Earth's crust along which movement may occur, causing earthquakes
Answer: *What is a fault?*

General Geography
Clue: Destructive physical event: flood, earthquake, hurricane
Answer: *What is a natural hazard?*

Places
Clue: The world's largest plain
Answer: *What is the West Siberian Plain?*

General Geography
Clue: The world's seven continents
Answer: *What are North and South America, Europe, Asia, Africa, Australia, Antarctica?*

General Geography
Clue: Theory that Earth's surface is divided into moving plates
Answer: *What is plate tectonics?*

General Geography
Clue: Westerly winds in a narrow, shallow stream in the upper troposphere
Answer: *What is the jet stream?*

Places
Clue: Area made up of the polar regions
Answer: *What is the ice cap?*

General Geography
Clue: This happens when water wears away soil and carries it away
Answer: *What is erosion?*

General Geography
Clue: Line of longitude 180° east and west of the Prime Meridian
Answer: *What is the International Date Line?*

General Geography
Clue: Precipitation from rain or snow melt that returns to streams and other water bodies
Answer: *What is runoff?*

Places
Clue: Biome with trees and woody vegetation; can be temperate, taiga, or tropical
Answer: *What is forest?*

General Geography
Clue: Theory that claims Earth's continents are constantly moving
Answer: *What is continental drift?*

General Geography
Clue: Altitude above which trees can no longer grow
Answer: *What is the timberline?*

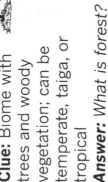

General Geography
Clue: Long-term trends in an area's weather conditions
Answer: *What is climate?*

Reproducible

CHAPTER 2

American History

Trading in Colonial Times

Objective

Students will understand the role played by the physical and social environment in the development of the Americas.

Trading card games put learning into a social context. In this game, students will learn that different cultures have their own beliefs, knowledge, values, and traditions. Students must strategize to trade cards and use deductive reasoning and negotiating skills as they explore the colonial period and various elements of society.

1. Engage students in a discussion about how they react to environmental challenges. Ask students: *What do you do when it snows? What do your parents do when your home loses power during storms? What comforts do you rely on when the weather changes?* Tell them that early American colonists faced many challenges in their new world. How they dealt with these challenges depended largely on their knowledge, available materials, and culture. Explain that early colonists did not have the comforts we have today. Survival was based on negotiating for goods, materials, and products needed to make life comfortable.

2. Use a figure, such as Elizabeth Lucas-Pinkney of South Carolina, to exemplify the colonial spirit. Explain that she took charge of her father's three plantations when he was called to the military. With the help of slaves, she grew crops such as alfalfa, ginger, cotton, indigo, and later, silkworms. Suggest some environmental challenges and difficulties that she might have encountered.

3. Ask students to identify regional crops that were traded between colonies, such as tobacco, corn, and wheat. Explain that colonists traded crops and other goods with each other and with Native Americans. Describe the barter system and how the relative values of goods and food crops were based on availability and need.

4. To prepare for the game, have students research the colonies. Ask them to write 15 questions and answers based on their research, such as: *What was the geography of the middle colonies?* Group students into teams of six and have them share their questions and answers. They will use these for the game.

Materials

- Colonial Game Board reproducible
- Colonial Trade Cards reproducible
- Colonial Characters Cards reproducible
- Colonial Elements Cards reproducible
- crayons or markers
- scissors
- glue
- manila folders
- index cards
- paper lunch bags
- reference materials, Internet access

5. Make enlarged copies of the **Colonial Game Board reproducible (page 20)**, one for each team and one to model the game. Select volunteers to color the model map and then have teams make their own. Give teams a copy of the **Colonial Trade Cards**, **Colonial Characters Cards**, and **Colonial Elements Cards reproducibles (pages 21–23)** and ask them to color and cut out the cards. Have students glue these cards to index cards and label the back of each card as *Trade, Characters,* or *Elements*.

6. Distribute a manila folder to each team to make their region cards. Explain that they should cut 12 horizontal strips (1" x 8") and then fold the strips in half. They should write the region—for example, *New England Colonies*—on the left and the colony of each region on the right. There will be 12 region cards, one for each colony.

7. Read the following instructions for the game. Ask volunteers to model one round while you assist as needed.
   a. Players choose the region in which they want to live and trade. There may be two players in one region, but they must choose separate colonies. Based on their research, have players choose the character card that matches their region.
   b. The goal is to get the most trade cards while traveling through the colonies. Players must answer a question and draw an elements card. All trades are made based on the situation described on the elements cards.
   c. Players shuffle and distribute the trade cards, which they keep next to them. They then shuffle the elements cards, place them in a stack on the game board, and place the folded region cards in a paper bag.
   d. The first player shakes the paper bag and pulls out a region card. The region and colony on the card is where the player places his or her character card. The player must answer the prepared question from the opponent who lives in that colony. (The player then places the region card back into the paper bag.)
   e. If the player answers the question correctly, he or she draws an elements card from the top of the stack. The player must then decide which trade to make based on the situation shown on the elements card. (Elements cards are critical to creating each trade scenario. For example, if a player draws a "storm," he or she should consider trading valuable goods for necessary food or candles.) A player's ability to make good trades helps to win the game.

Note: If the player already has an item(s) on the trade card, he or she must still make a trade. Players may trade goods for less than they are worth to make alliances.

    f. If the player answers the question incorrectly, he or she draws an elements card and then gives up a trade card to the questioner, receiving nothing in return.

    g. Play moves to the player on the right, who then begins the process all over again by drawing a region card from the bag.

    h. Players who lose all their trade cards are out of the game. The player with the most trade cards wins!

8. Allow groups to play the game on their own. Circulate around the room to answer any questions. Remind players that they must master their negotiating skills in order to win. While the object of the game is to gain items to survive, some opponents might block trades. Tell students that to combat this, players can make alliances and combine resources to overpower an adversary.

9. After students play the game, ask them if negotiating for goods helped them understand what it took to survive in the colonies. For example: *Were you able to understand the complexities of living in hostile environments? What would you do differently?*

Colonial Game Board

New England Colonies: Massachusetts, New Hampshire, Rhode Island
Middle Colonies: New York, Pennsylvania, New Jersey, Delaware
Southern Colonies: Maryland, Virginia, North Carolina, South Carolina, Georgia

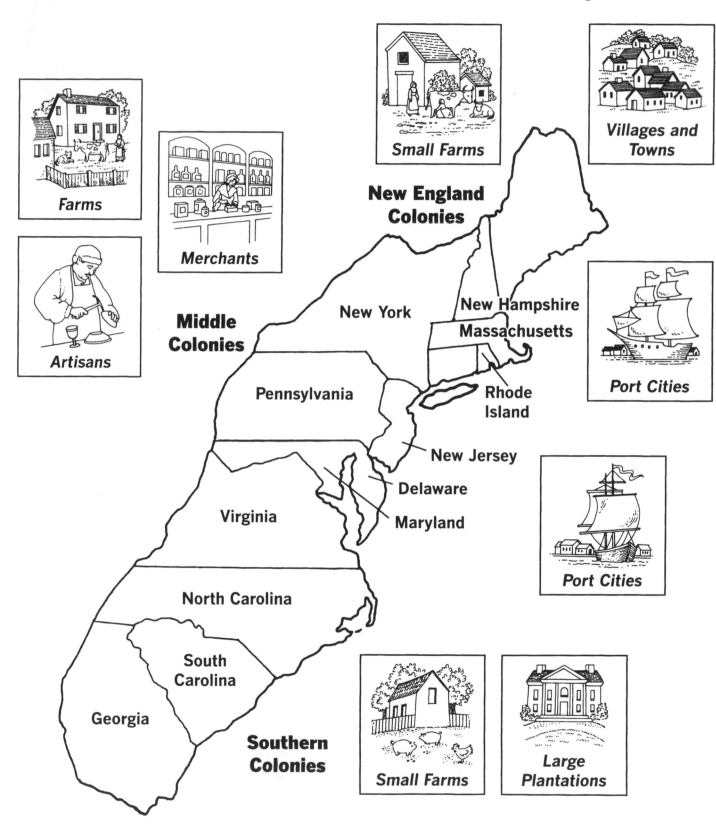

Farms

Merchants

Artisans

Small Farms

Villages and Towns

New England Colonies

Middle Colonies

New York

New Hampshire
Massachusetts

Pennsylvania

Rhode Island

Port Cities

New Jersey

Delaware

Maryland

Virginia

Port Cities

North Carolina

South Carolina

Georgia

Southern Colonies

Small Farms

Large Plantations

Colonial Trade Cards

Dried Cod	Salt Beef	Pork	Hemp
Linen	Cattle	Timber	Land
Tobacco	Beaver	Blankets	Cooking Pots
Beads	Corn	Squash	Pottery
Candles	Firewood	Rice	Indigo

Colonial Characters Cards

Native American

Native American

Small Farm Owner

Small Farm Owner

Merchant

Merchant

Fisherman

Carpenter

Candle Maker

Southern Plantation Owner

Southern Plantation Owner

Indentured Servant

Colonial Elements Cards

 Storm: You cannot trade, travel, fish, or farm. Lose one card to stay in the colony.

 Storm: You need candles, firewood, shelter, and food. Make a trade for each.

 Rain: Your wagon is stuck in mud. Make a trade for a team of horses to pull you out.

 Rain: You run out of candles. Make a trade.

 Cold Weather: It is cold. Lose one turn.

 Cold Weather: It is cold. Trade for a blanket.

 Hot Summer: You are hungry. Trade something for dried cod.

 Hot Summer: Sudden summer storm hits. Lose one trade card.

 Spring Day: It is a good day for hunting. Take a trade card from an opponent.

 Spring Day: You need supplies for summer. Trade three cards for goods.

 Fire: A brush fire starts. Lose two trade cards.

 Fire: A fire breaks out in your home. Give away three trade cards.

 Wind: A great wind knocks over your cooking pottery. Trade to replenish.

 Wind: The wind keeps you from traveling. Lose one trade card to stay in the colony.

 Hurricane: A hurricane keeps you from traveling. Lose one card to stay in the colony.

 Hurricane: A hurricane sweeps away some of your belongings. Lose two cards.

 Snow: You are snowbound. Lose one trade card to stay in the colony.

 Snow: It is snowing, but you have caught extra beaver. Trade for winter items.

Industrial Revolution Charades

Materials
- Industrial Revolution Inventions reproducibles
- timer

Objective
Students will understand the importance of major inventions of the Industrial Revolution.

Playing Charades inspires cooperative learning and allows students to process information creatively. Normally shy students will come out of their shells and feel like part of the group. This game introduces inventions developed during the Industrial Revolution, but the game works well with any topic.

1. Ahead of time, create a class set of game cards. Photocopy and cut out the cards from the **Industrial Revolution Inventions reproducibles (pages 27–28)**.

2. Initiate a discussion about the Industrial Revolution in the United States. Encourage students to consider the influence of inventions such as the telegraph and the telephone. Explore the positive effects that the Industrial Revolution had on society. These might include economic expansion, introduction of factories and the assembly line, efficient production of goods and materials, and the development of electricity. Write students' responses on the board.

3. Then ask for some drawbacks of the Industrial Revolution. These might include uncontrolled urbanization, child labor, and poor working conditions.

4. Divide the class into nine study groups. Give each group one Industrial Revolution Inventions card and allow time for research and discussion about assigned inventions. On each card, have students write a brief description of the invention and how it is (or was) used. Ask students to share their findings with classmates.

5. Collect the cards from student groups. Explain that the cards will be used to play a game similar to Charades. Ask a volunteer to explain and model how to play Charades and allow the class to guess what is being acted out.

6. Then share the following game rules with the class. Charades is played with two competing teams racing against time. Each player draws a card and gets two minutes to act out the invention for teammates without using words. The team who guesses the most inventions wins the game.
   - No words are allowed.
   - Players may pantomime what the invention does, how the invention is used, or the invention itself.
   - Players may not spell out the name of the invention.
   - Players may not draw the invention.
   - Teams alternate until each team member has had an opportunity to pantomime.

Standard Signals to Use During Pantomime
   - **Location:** Make a circle with one hand and point as if pointing to a map.
   - **Correct:** Point to your nose and the player who has given a correct answer.
   - **Sounds Like:** Pull on your earlobe with one hand.
   - **Longer Answer:** Pretend to stretch a piece of elastic.
   - **Shorter Answer:** Push hands together.
   - **Getting Warm:** Wave hands toward yourself.
   - **Not Even Close:** Wave hands away from yourself.
   - **First Word/Second Word:** Hold out one or two fingers.

7. Ask for three volunteers to model a round of the game. Have a volunteer draw a card without letting the others see. Give the student a minute to think about how he or she will pantomime the invention. Set the timer for two minutes and tell the student to begin. Tell the other two volunteers to call out words they think the student is acting out. Have them continue guessing until someone guesses the correct answer or time expires.

8. Ask if there are any questions. Divide the class into two teams and begin play. Monitor students closely to make sure they are following the rules and using the correct signals.

9. After the game, ask students why they think each invention was so important when it was first created. The sewing machine, for example, saved hours of work for women who had always sewed the family's clothes by hand. The invention made clothes cheaper for the mass market.

10. For future rounds of the game, have students create more invention cards. See the following list for ideas.

Industrial Revolution Inventions	
Invention	**Date**
Spinning Jenny	1764
Water Frame	1769
Steam Engine	1775
Power Loom	1785
Cotton Gin	1793
Rail Locomotive	1804
Telegraph	1836
Camera	1839
Sewing Machine	1844
Transatlantic Cable	1866
Telephone	1876
Phonograph	1877
Lightbulb	1879
Internal Combustion Engine	1886
Electric Motor	1888
Diesel Engine	1892
First Airplane	1903
Model T Ford	1908
Model T Assembly line	1913

Extended Learning

- Play Paired Charades by letting two students act out a scene related to the Industrial Revolution. For example, a team could pantomime a scene showing the Wright brothers at Kitty Hawk.

- Have students play Tableau Charades, in which a group forms a scene and stays perfectly still, while one member of the group responds to guesses. Players try to guess what the scene represents.

- Invite students to play a game based on more recent inventions, such as the computer, cell phone, television, video game, MP3 player, and so on.

Industrial Revolution Inventions

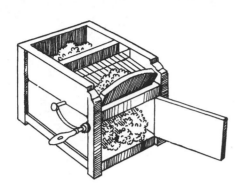

Cotton Gin (1793)

_____

_____

_____

_____

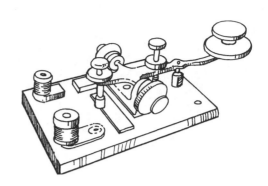

Telegraph (1836)

_____

_____

_____

_____

Sewing Machine (1844)

_____

_____

_____

_____

Telephone (1876)

_____

_____

_____

_____

Industrial Revolution Inventions

Phonograph (1877)

_____

_____

_____

_____

Lightbulb (1879)

_____

_____

_____

_____

Electric Motor (1888)

_____

_____

_____

_____

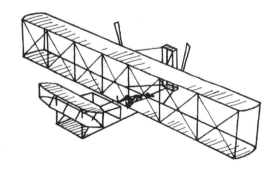

Airplane (1903)

_____

_____

_____

_____

Go West!

Objective

Students will identify natural land features encountered by pioneers moving West.

Played in the style of Go Fish!, this fun visual game reinforces learning about westward expansion. Students are "exposed" to various climactic and environmental challenges to gain an understanding of what the pioneers faced while traveling the Oregon Trail.

1. Provide students with some background information about the Oregon Trail: *During the Great Migration of 1843, the pioneers of the Oregon Trail traveled over half the continent to reach their destination. Their travels took them through land we now know as Missouri, Kansas, Nebraska, Wyoming, Idaho, and Oregon.* Using a wall map of the United States, mark the areas where the Oregon Trail began and ended.

2. Ask students to define the term *Manifest Destiny (the philosophy that the United States deserved to expand the nation from the Atlantic Ocean to the Pacific Ocean).* Ask students if they have visited places along the Oregon Trail. Allow them to share their experiences.

3. Tell students that the first organized wagon train on the Oregon Trail began in Elm Grove, Missouri, on May 16, 1842. It was made up of more than 100 pioneers, including children. Discuss with students what it might have been like crossing the continent. Ask: *What were some of the challenges pioneers faced? How would you prepare for the trip? What food and supplies would you bring? What would the same trip be like today?* Tell students they will play a game about the Oregon Trail.

4. Divide the class into teams of three to six students each. Make four copies each of the **Go West! Game Cards reproducibles (pages 31–32)** for each team. Ask team members to color and cut out the pictures and glue them to separate index cards to make a deck of 72 cards.

5. Explain that this game is played like Go Fish! Ask for volunteers who have played Go Fish! to model one round while you explain the rules of the game.
   a. The object of the game is for players to get rid of all their cards by creating matched sets, four images per set.
   b. The dealer deals five cards to each player.

Materials

- Go West! Game Cards reproducibles
- thin graphic tape in two different colors
- United States wall map
- scissors
- index cards
- glue sticks
- crayons or markers

c. Player 1 looks at his or her cards and chooses an image. Player 1 then asks any other player (Player 2) for a card with that image: *Do you have oxen?* Player 1 cannot ask for a card that is not in his or her own hand.

d. If Player 2 has a card with that image, he or she must give it to Player 1.

e. If Player 2 does not have the requested card, he or she says: *Go West!*, and Player 1 must draw a card from the deck.

f. Players may place four matching cards on the table at any time during their turn.

g. The game continues until someone runs out of cards or until there are no cards left to draw. The player with the most matches wins!

6. Answer any questions students may have, and then invite students to play on their own. Circulate around the room to ensure students are following the rules and exhibiting good sportsmanship.

7. After students finish playing, ask them to name any additional items they might need to travel the Oregon Trail, such as books, toys, writing instruments, and lanterns.

Extended Learning

- Read excerpts of first-hand accounts from those who experienced the trials and tribulations of traveling the Oregon Trail. Consider the writings of Narcissa Whitman or Catherine Sager Pringle. Full text of their diaries and letters can be found online at The Oregon Trail Diaries: *www.isu.edu/~trinmich/00.n.diaries.html.*

- Suggest that students put the diaries and letters from the Oregon Trail into script form and create their own plays. Encourage the use of props and sets. Allow time in class for students to perform their skits. If you wish, invite other classes to watch the performances.

Chimney Rock, Nebraska

Devil's Gate, Wyoming

Craters of the Moon, Idaho

The Dalles, Oregon

Whitman Mission, Washington

Council Bluffs, Iowa

Independence, Missouri

Alcove Spring, Kansas

Mountains

Go West! Game Cards

Dust	Rivers	Native Americans
Oxen and Conestoga Wagon	Protection	Tools
Food	Pots and Pans	Blankets and Clothing

"Dust Bowl" Coin Pitch

Objective
Students will understand the negative impact of overdevelopment.

Materials
- United States Map
- various colors of chalk
- masking tape
- paper bag
- pennies
- index cards

Physical games for the classroom encourage active processing of content on different levels. Active involvement promotes better retention. This coin pitch game is a fun, active, outdoor game that blends challenge and novelty.

1. Provide students with some background information about the Dust Bowl: *When settlers moved into the Great Plains, they plowed through millions of acres of grasslands and turned it into farmland. In the 1930s, an eight-year drought devastated the region. Warm winds dried the exposed soil into a fine dust. These elements came together to create the Dust Bowl.*

2. On a United States map, ask students to identify the Dust Bowl region (included these Great Plains states: Texas, South Dakota, Kansas, Arkansas, and Oklahoma).

3. Divide the class into several study groups. Give students time to research and write ten questions and answers regarding the Dust Bowl on index cards. Have them write questions on one side and answers on the other. For example:

   Question: *What was the Dust Bowl?*

   Answer: *A region of the American Great Plains that was stricken by drought.*

   Question: *What was Black Sunday?*

   Answer: *The day dust blizzards turned the air so black that it looked as if day turned into night.*

4. Once groups have completed their research, take time to review all of the questions and answers with the class. Then show the groups how to create their game board outside. Mark off a 5' x 5' square with tape or chalk. Divide that square into five smaller boxes to represent five of the Great Plains states: Texas, South Dakota, Kansas, Arkansas, and Oklahoma. Ask volunteers to label each box with a state name and then draw a simple farmhouse in the center of each box. Then draw a line about five feet back from the game board. This is where students will stand when tossing the coin.

5. Place the question/answer cards in a paper bag. Then divide the class into groups of four. Each group then divides into two teams of two. Invite volunteers to help you model the game while you explain the rules.
   a. The object of the game is to answer a question correctly and then toss a coin onto a chosen farmhouse in a Dust Bowl state.
   b. The first player draws a question card from the bag. He or she must answer it correctly to earn a toss.
   c. If the player answers correctly, he or she must "call" the state before attempting the toss. Players may not step over the line while tossing the coin.
   d. If the coin lands in the appropriate state box, the player gets a point for his or her team. The player then crosses out that box on the game board.
   e. If the coin lands outside the state box, it does not count, and play passes to the other team.
   f. Play continues until all states have been crossed out. The team with the most points wins.

6. Answer any questions about the game before the class separates into teams to play on their own. Provide students with chalk to create their own game boards and monitor them as they play. Assist students as needed.

7. After the game, have students review the causes that led to the Dust Bowl. Then ask if they can name any examples today of overdevelopment of natural lands. Suggest places such as the tropical rainforests in South America.

Extended Learning

- Have the class read John Steinbeck's novel, *Grapes of Wrath*, or show the film adaptation in class.

- Ask students to read about the effects of the Dust Bowl, such as the economic activity of the region before and after the drought, on the National Archives Web site: *www.archives.gov/research/arc/education*.

978-1-4129-5952-0

Stand Up for Civil Rights

Objective

Students will recognize the roots and influences of the civil rights movement in America.

Games encourage active listening skills, and active listeners enjoy more success in school. Played similarly to Bingo, this game requires students to listen carefully and act on what they hear. Use this game to reinforce learning in any topic of study.

1. Initiate a discussion with students about the civil rights movement. Explain that the United States changed dramatically as a result and the struggles of activists affected laws and influenced generations to come. Ask students how the effects of the civil rights movement can still be seen and felt today.

2. Point out that in our country's recent history, African Americans, women, and other groups have had to fight for rights described in the Constitution. Remind students that people began fighting for their rights more than a century ago. Recall the efforts of Elizabeth Cady Stanton for women's rights and of Frederick Douglass for the abolishment of slavery. Explain that the actions of such figures resulted in amendments to the Constitution, but many problems were not addressed until the 1950s and 1960s.

3. Give students copies of the **Civil Rights Caller's List reproducibles (pages 37–38)**. Explain that the reproducibles will be used to play a game similar to Bingo. Allow them time to study the topics on the list, including the NAACP, Rosa Parks, Martin Luther King Jr., and important people from the women's rights movement.

4. Once students have had time to study the information, give them two copies of the **Civil Rights Answers List reproducible (page 39)** and one copy of the **Civil Rights Game Board reproducible (page 40)**.

5. Explain to students that they will prepare their own game board and markers. Hand out sheets of colored paper and ask students to cut them into small squares. Then have them cut out the boxes on the Civil Rights Answers List reproducible and glue them in random order on the game board.

6. Ahead of time, prepare a game board to display on a transparency. Model how the game is played while you explain the following directions. Ask a student volunteer to read a few questions from the Civil Rights Caller's List in random order. Mark off the answers on the game board.
   a. This game is played in the style of Bingo. The object of the game is to fill a horizontal, diagonal, or vertical line with colored paper squares.
   b. Players listen as the "caller" reads questions.
   c. Once a question is read, players look for the answer on their game board. If the answer is there, they cover it with a colored paper square.
   d. When colored squares make a horizontal, diagonal, or vertical line, the player shouts: *Stand up for civil rights!*
   e. Check to make sure all the answers have been marked correctly. If all answers are correct, that player wins the game. If not, continue play until someone else marks a complete row.

7. Once you make sure that students understand the game, play one round. You will be the caller in the first round. The winner then becomes the new caller for the next round, and so on. Check the winner's answers using the Civil Rights Caller's List.

8. After playing several rounds, ask students if they believe more work needs to be done to guarantee civil rights for all people. Ask what they would do if suddenly they could not eat in certain restaurants or if they could not freely voice their opinions.

Extended Learning

- Focus on more specific aspects of the civil rights movement, such as the Montgomery Bus Boycott and Rosa Parks. Create new questions and game boards for these topics.

- Tell students that the Constitution and the Bill of Rights protect the rights of all citizens. Ask volunteers to read the Bill of Rights and the 13th, 14th, 15th, 19th, and 24th amendments to the Constitution. Discuss the language in the documents. Ask students to share what it means to have rights as a United States citizen.

Civil Rights Caller's List

Question: Who wouldn't give her seat to a white man, triggering the Montgomery Bus Boycott?
Answer: Rosa Parks

Question: What laws enforced "separate but equal" status for African Americans?
Answer: Jim Crow laws

Question: What form of non-violent protest involves one or more people sitting down?
Answer: Sit-ins

Question: Which amendment to the Constitution protects a citizen's right to vote, regardless of race, color, or condition?
Answer: 15th Amendment

Question: Who was one of the first African American students to attempt to enter Little Rock Central High School on September 4, 1957?
Answer: Elizabeth Eckford

Question: Which amendment to the Constitution guarantees women the right to vote?
Answer: 19th Amendment

Question: Which amendment to the Constitution prohibits taxing of polling places?
Answer: 24th Amendment

Question: What protest intended to stop racial segregation on public transit systems in 1955?
Answer: Montgomery Bus Boycott

Question: What is one of the United States' oldest, most influential civil rights organizations?
Answer: NAACP

Question: Which amendment to the Constitution contains "due process" and "equal protection" clauses?
Answer: 14th Amendment

Question: At age 35, which famous civil rights leader was the youngest American to receive the Nobel Peace Prize?
Answer: Martin Luther King Jr.

Question: Which city and state are known to be the first capital of the confederacy and the primary site of the civil rights movement?
Answer: Montgomery, Alabama

Question: What political rally or march took place on August 28, 1963?
Answer: March on Washington, DC

Civil Rights Caller's List

Question: What phrase regarding equality appears in the opening of the Declaration of Independence?
Answer: *"All men are created equal"*

Question: What term defines the separation of different races?
Answer: *Segregation*

Question: What feminist group was founded by Betty Friedan in 1966?
Answer: *National Organization for Women (NOW)*

Question: Which amendment to the Constitution outlaws slavery?
Answer: *13th Amendment*

Question: When did the Jim Crow era begin?
Answer: *1876*

Question: What documents are the foundation of American democracy?
Answer: *The Declaration of Independence and the Constitution*

Question: In 1979, this famous woman suffragist became the first woman depicted on U.S. currency, the dollar coin.
Answer: *Susan B. Anthony*

Question: What historic speech did Martin Luther King Jr. give at the Lincoln Memorial during the March on Washington?
Answer: *"I Have a Dream"*

Question: Who was the 35th President of the United States?
Answer: *President John F. Kennedy*

Question: Name a law that forbids men and women to receive different wages for the same job.
Answer: *Equal Pay Act*

Question: Who wrote the groundbreaking book *The Feminine Mystique* in 1963?
Answer: *Betty Friedan*

Question: Which civil rights movement dealt with issues such as reproductive rights, equal pay, and maternity leave?
Answer: *Feminist movement*

Question: What is a population of human beings whose members identify with each other based on ancestry or genealogy?
Answer: *Ethnic group*

Civil Rights Answers List

Rosa Parks	Jim Crow laws	Sit-ins	15th Amendment
Elizabeth Eckford	19th Amendment	24th Amendment	Montgomery Bus Boycott
NAACP	Susan B. Anthony	14th Amendment	Betty Friedan
Montgomery, Alabama	March on Washington, DC	"All men are created equal"	Segregation
National Organization for Women (NOW)	13th Amendment	1876	The Declaration of Independence and the Constitution
Martin Luther King Jr.	"I Have a Dream"	President John F. Kennedy	Equal Pay Act
Feminist movement	Ethnic group		

Civil Rights Game Board

Directions: Glue the boxes from the Answers List on the game board in random order. When you cover one horizontal, vertical, or diagonal row, shout: *Stand up for civil rights!*

WE SHALL OVERCOME	THE PERSONAL IS POLITICAL	SNCC	Women Make Policy Not Coffee		JOBS NOW!

CHAPTER 3

World History

"Historical Figures" 20 Questions

Objectives
Students will understand how individuals shaped history.
Students will recognize different historical points of view.

Materials
- Historical Figures Cards reproducibles
- scissors
- paper lunch bag
- reference materials

History comes to life when we recognize elements that humans have in common, regardless of time and place. In this game, played like 20 Questions, students try to guess the historical figure by asking questions, following clues, and learning facts. This game can be played using any historical figures.

1. Explain that people in the past have things in common with people today and faced similar challenges. Invite volunteers to share about the lives of older family members, such as grandparents or great-grandparents. For example: *My great-grandfather only went to school through the sixth grade because he had to work on the family farm. I'm lucky because I can stay in school. But when I grow up, I want to help my family, too.*

2. Ask students what they know about a well-known historical figure, such as Thomas Jefferson. Write their responses on the board. Explain that Jefferson came from a large family, went to college, and practiced law. He married and had six children. Ask volunteers to name some of the jobs that Jefferson had. Responses may include: *Governor of Virginia, Minister to France, Secretary of State under George Washington,* and *President of the United States*. Point out that Jefferson was similar to some politicians today. He favored states' rights and believed in the separation of church and state. Encourage students to name other similarities.

3. Prepare a class set of the **Historical Figures Cards reproducibles (pages 44–45)** by photocopying and cutting out the cards. (You may want to use different historical figures, depending on what your class is studying.) Display the cards for the class, pointing out that each card includes three key facts about that person.

4. Give students time to research the historical figures and come up with additional facts. Remind them to note such details as where and how the person lived, what jobs the person had, and what made the person historically important. They can write the facts on the backs of the cards, or they can glue the cutouts to index cards to make more room for writing. Place all the finished cards in a paper bag.

5. Tell the class that they will play a guessing game similar to 20 Questions. Divide the class into two teams. Ask for a volunteer from each team to be the historical "expert." The expert will secretly choose one of the historical figures cards from the bag. The rest of the team will ask questions.

6. Explain that each team will try to guess the historical figure by asking the expert "yes" or "no" questions, one at a time. For example: *Is this person a man? Has he ever been president of the United States?* Students can ask up to 20 questions. If the team doesn't guess correctly, the other team gets a chance. Each correct guess earns one point.

7. Review the rules with the class. Model the game one time, with you acting as the expert. Invite the whole class to ask questions.

Rules of the Game

- Players must ask a "yes" or "no" question. Once each question is asked and answered, the expert moves to the next student.

- To make a guess, players must raise their hand and wait to be called on.

- Players cannot ask a question and guess the identity of the historical figure in the same turn.

- If players think they know the answer, they must make a guess instead of asking a question.

- When a player guesses correctly, he or she receives one point and becomes the expert for the next round.

- If 20 questions are asked without a correct guess, the expert receives two points and continues as the expert for another round.

- Fibbing or misleading classmates is not allowed!

978-1-4129-5952-0

8. After playing several rounds of the game, invite students to discuss which historical figure they think is most important and why. Encourage them to research historical figures from various time periods and play the game again.

Extended Learning

- Have students choose their favorite historical figure for an oral report. Encourage them to be creative about how they present the information. For example, students may dress up in a costume and act out information from that person's perspective.

- You may want to group the cards into categories, such as by nation or gender. Make your own cards that focus on a unit the class is currently studying, such as explorers or scientists.

- Create cards in pairs, such as Lewis and Clark, Antony and Cleopatra, and Aristotle and Plato. Use the cards in a memory matching game by placing them facedown in a grid format. Have students turn over two cards at a time and try to make matches.

- Have students create their own set of historical figures cards to use as flashcard study aids.

- Explain to students: *Through the ages, people have asked what makes a person great, famous, or infamous. Is it environmental, educational, spiritual, or cultural? Time and place? Perhaps it is none of these or a combination of them all.* Use each card to open a discussion about why that person has been remembered.

Historical Figures Cards

Julius Caesar
- Roman military and political leader
- Proclaimed dictator for life
- Assassinated by friend, Marcus Brutus, on the "Ides of March" (March 15)

Murasaki Shikibu
- Maid of honor in the imperial court of Japan during the Heian period
- Given a "male" education by her father and hailed as an intellectual
- Wrote one of the most famous novels in early history, *The Tale of the Ginja*

Montezuma
- Ruler of the Aztec empire
- Expanded the Aztec empire to the south of Mexico
- Held hostage in his own palace and temple by the Spaniards

Cleopatra
- Last pharaoh of Egypt
- Partnered with Julius Caesar, and later, with Mark Antony
- Her reign marked the end of the Hellenistic Era and start of the Roman Era in Egypt

Galileo Galilei
- Italian Renaissance scientist
- Supported Copernicus's theories that the sun was the center of the galaxy
- Ordered to stand trial for heresy

Queen Elizabeth I
- Queen of England and final monarch of the Tudor dynasty
- Only surviving child of King Henry VIII
- Reigned for 44 years

John Q. Adams
- Sixth President of the United States
- Son of second President, John Adams
- Formulated the Monroe Doctrine

Hammurabi
- First king of the Babylonian empire
- Secured his kingdom by heightening city walls and developing public works
- Wrote the first code of laws recorded in history

Mahatma Ghandi
- Major 20th century leader of India and Indian Independence Movement
- Pioneer of *Satyagraha*, the resistance of tyranny through mass civil disobedience
- Known worldwide for inducing change through peaceful protest

King Henry VIII
- King of England and Ireland from 1509 until his death in 1547
- Infamous for his six marriages, he was head of the Church of England
- Brought Protestantism to England; helped break with Roman Catholic Church

Historical Figures Cards

Ramses the Great
- Reigned as pharaoh of Egypt for 66 years
- Turned Egypt into a country of peace and prosperity
- Married to Queen Nefertari and entombed in the Valley of the Kings

Alexander the Great
- Great military leader and King of Macedonia
- Tutored as a boy by Aristotle
- Conquered most of the world known to the Greeks

Aristotle
- Greek philosopher and student of Plato
- Wrote on subjects such as physics, metaphysics, poetry, politics, and ethics
- His philosophy remains the foundation of Western thought

George Washington
- Led the Continental Army to victory in the American Revolutionary War
- Presided over the Constitutional Convention in 1787
- The first elected President of the United States of America

Thomas Jefferson
- Third President of the United States
- Principle author of the Declaration of Independence
- Bought land in North America from France, which became known as the Louisiana Purchase

Queen Isabella of Spain
- Queen Regent of Castile and Leon; wife of King Ferdinand
- Conquered the Moorish-held Kingdom of Granada
- Began the Golden Age of exploration and colonization for Spain

Lewis and Clark
- Led an expedition across the United States to the Pacific Ocean and back
- Recruited a party of 29 men for the Corps of Discovery
- First citizens of the United States to cross the Continental Divide

Sacagawea
- Vital member of Lewis and Clark expedition
- Shoshone Indian, kidnapped by Hidatsa Indians when she was ten years old
- Helped save important materials and documents from a boat during the Lewis and Clark expedition

Joan of Arc
- During the Middle Ages, hero of France and saint of the Catholic Church
- Claimed she had orders from God to recover France from English domination
- Captured by the English, tried as a heretic, and burned at the stake

Martin Luther King Jr.
- Leader in the American civil rights movement
- Youngest American awarded the Nobel Peace Prize
- Assassinated in Memphis, Tennessee, on April 4, 1968

Middle Ages Trivia Board Game

Objectives

Students will learn how feudalism was influenced by physical geography, the role and limits of feudal society, and the foundation of political order. Students will understand how feudal systems developed and affected the European economy.

By generating questions together in small groups, students recall information, solve problems, and explore topics in-depth. This board game helps students understand feudalism and the nuances of society during Europe's Middle Ages.

Part 1: Preparing for the Game

1. Access students' prior knowledge by asking them to share what they know about the Middle Ages. Suggest the following topics for discussion: *Why did warring principalities and governments fight? How did geography, resources, and economies play a role in the development of the Middle Ages? How was feudalism in Europe directly related to the fall of Rome?* Expand the discussion to include how the citizens were affected. Ask: *Did gender, education, and social status play a role? If so, how? What impact did the development of the trades and guilds have on society?* Write students' responses on the board.

2. Explain to students that they are going to play a trivia board game about the Middle Ages. Display one of the **Serf Cards reproducibles (pages 50–52)** on a transparency. Point out that the cards are divided into categories.

3. Divide the class into groups of six. Pass out copies of the Serf Cards reproducibles to each group. Have students cut out and glue the cards to index cards for durability. Ask them to write the category on the backs of the cards and then separate the cards into categories.

Materials

- Middle Ages Trivia Game Board reproducible
- Serf Cards reproducibles
- Holy Grail Cards reproducible
- overhead projector and transparencies
- small chips or other game pieces
- dice
- poster board
- index cards
- scissors
- glue
- markers
- colored art paper
- paper lunch bags or small boxes
- reference materials on the Middle Ages

4. Provide materials for student groups to research and write ten questions and answers that they will add to the serf cards. Remind students that they should keep the categories in mind as they write. For example, a question for the category *Development of Feudalism* could be: *Why were serfs important?* Answer: *Serfs were important because they worked the land and built the economy.* Students may also use the topics written on the board during the opening discussion.

5. Then distribute a copy of the **Holy Grail Cards reproducible (page 53)** to each group. Have groups cut out and glue these cards to index cards as well, labeling the backs *Holy Grail*. Explain that holy grail cards contain questions at a higher level of difficulty. As with the serf cards, have student groups write ten difficult questions and answers to add to the holy grail cards.

6. Finally, distribute markers and sheets of paper. Students will draw a variety of coats of arms, similar to the examples shown at the bottom of page 48. Each coat of arms should be about the size of a small sticky note. Have students collect all coats of arms in a box or bag to use during the game.

7. Give each group a copy of the **Middle Ages Trivia Game Board reproducible (page 49)**. Students will use this as a guide to draw their own game board on poster board. Encourage them to be creative by adding graphics and designs from the Middle Ages. Once the game boards are completed, place all the cards in their designated locations.

Part 2: Let the Games Begin!

1. Read the following directions to the class while modeling the game with a couple of volunteers. Answer any questions as you go along. The object of the game is to move along the cobblestone road by correctly answering questions. For each correct answer, the player wins a coat of arms. Whoever reaches the castle and answers the holy grail question correctly wins the game.
   a. All play begins at the center on the castle.
   b. Players throw two dice and move their game piece in any direction around the board.
   c. Wherever the game piece lands, players must answer a serf card question from that section of the board. The opponent to the right draws a serf card and reads the question to the player. (Place used cards at the bottom of the stack.)
   d. If players answer correctly, they win a coat of arms and then roll the dice for another turn.

e. If players do not answer correctly, the next player gets a turn.

f. Note that players cannot move over a bridge to the castle until they have traveled once around the cobblestone road and collected at least eight coats of arms.

g. Once players are ready to move to the castle, they must land directly on a bridge space. If they overshoot the bridge, they must answer a serf card question from the category where they land and try again during their next turn.

h. In order to win, a player who moves up the bridge must correctly answer a holy grail question. If the answer is incorrect, he or she stays there and waits for the next turn.

2. Invite volunteers to model the game for a few minutes. Once students understand how to play, have them break up into their groups and start a game.

3. After the game, discuss with students the different levels and roles of feudalism in the Middle Ages. Write their ideas on the board by dividing them into the categories used while playing the game.

Extended Learning

Ask students if they know of any countries today that are in the midst of governmental and cultural redevelopment after a long period of leadership by one group. Initiate a discussion on the challenges and struggles these countries have encountered.

Middle Ages Trivia Game Board

Directions: Use this diagram to create your own game board. Color and decorate the game board with pictures and designs from the Middle Ages.

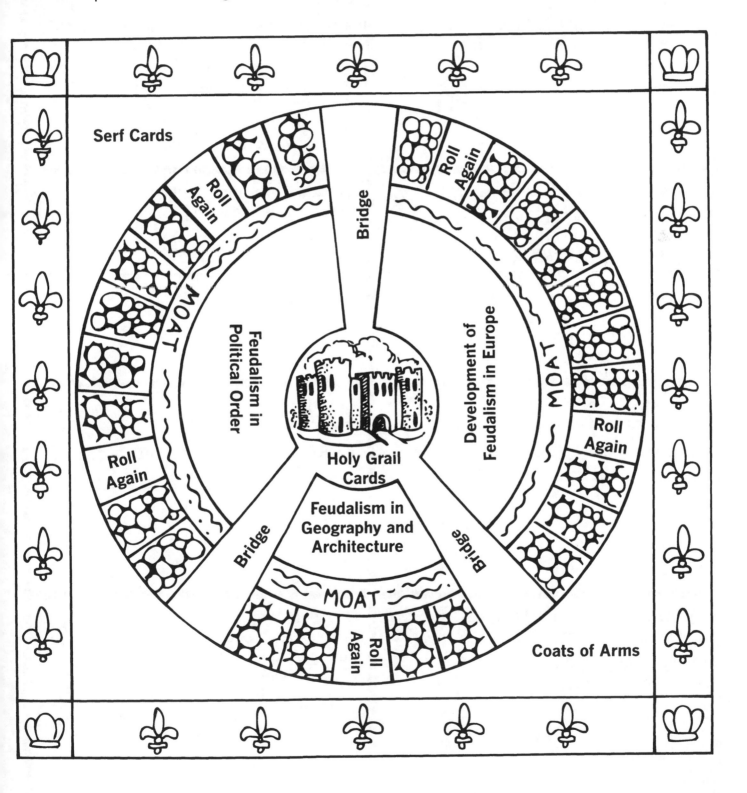

Serf Cards: Development of Feudalism

Question: Name one reason why feudalism emerged in Europe.

Answer: *The disintegration of the Roman Empire; the invasion of Germanic tribes; the breakdown of central governments*

Question: Who was William the Conqueror?

Answer: *He invaded England to claim the throne from the Saxon king during the Battle of Hastings. He was crowned King of England in 1066. He secured the beginnings of the feudal system in England.*

Question: Who was Charlemagne?

Answer: *The most powerful ruler during the Middle Ages; he conquered the Saxons, other Germanic tribes, and Muslims in Spain. He forced his conquered people to accept Christianity.*

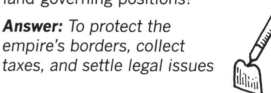

Question: Why did Charlemagne reward his nobles with land-governing positions?

Answer: *To protect the empire's borders, collect taxes, and settle legal issues*

Question: In which country did feudalism first begin?

Answer: *France*

Question: Who brought feudalism to England?

Answer: *William the Conqueror*

Question: What was the purpose of feudalism in Europe?

Answer: *To give the people stability and order*

Question: Who promoted learning and scholarship during Europe's early Middle Ages?

Answer: *Charlemagne*

Serf Cards: Feudalism in Geography and Architecture

Question: In the Middle Ages, what did kings, lords, nobles and even the church fight for?

Answer: Land and power

Question: Where did the first Crusaders of the Middle Ages travel?

Answer: Jerusalem

Question: Where did the bubonic plague begin in Europe?

Answer: Italy

Question: Where did Gothic cathedral designs develop?

Answer: France

Question: Name two reasons why the Crusades began.

Answer: The Holy Lands had been captured by the Muslim Turks. Christians had been fighting in Europe. Pope Urban believed it was time to fight the enemy in the East.

Question: Where did feudalism first spread?

Answer: Feudalism spread from France to Spain and Italy, and later, to Eastern Europe. William the Conqueror brought his Frankish form of feudalism to England in 1066.

Question: What new style of architecture developed during this time?

Answer: Gothic architecture

Question: What was the symbolism of Gothic architecture?

Answer: The architecture reflected the way people thought of God. The use of light in the new style of windows symbolized heaven.

Serf Cards: Feudalism in Political Order

Question: Who were vassals?

Answer: People who received land from a lord because of their loyalty or service

Question: Where did the largest peasant revolt begin?

Answer: England

Question: Why did thousands of peasants begin a revolt against the nobility toward the end of the Middle Ages?

Answer: They grew tired of paying high taxes and serving their lords.

Question: What was the first representative government in England called?

Answer: Parliament

Question: What was "common law"?

Answer: A new system of laws practiced throughout a kingdom

Question: What was the political role of the church?

Answer: The church fought to have independent rule over the kings and their kingdoms.

Question: Why was the alliance between the church and small duchies important?

Answer: They mutually benefited from each other through protection of land, royal titles, and riches.

Question: Name a person ordained as a saint during the Middle Ages.

Answer: St. Benedict, St. Augustine of Hippo, St. Augustine of Canterbury, Joan of Arc, St. Francis of Assisi, Hildegard of Bingen, St. Thomas Aquinas

Holy Grail Cards

Question: Who was Joan of Arc?

Answer: *A young French girl who believed God told her to lead the French army to victory. She was captured by the English, convicted of heresy, and burned at the stake.*

Question: Where did the first university in Europe open during the Middle Ages?

Answer: *Bologna, Italy*

Question: What ended feudalism?

Answer: *A few powerful monarchs breaking down local organizations; the rise of towns and the growth of the middle class*

Question: What was the Domesday Book?

Answer: *An accounting book that collected information about England's wealth*

Question: What two branches of English Parliament were developed in the Middle Ages?

Answer: *House of Commons and House of Lords*

Question: What was the meaning behind the rose windows in cathedrals?

Answer: *To honor Mary, the mother of Jesus*

Question: What new English weapons were used against armor during the Hundred Years' War?

Answer: *Guns, gunpowder, and cannon*

Question: Who destroyed the great library of Constantinople?

Answer: *The Crusaders*

Question: Where did the second Crusade go?

Answer: *To Antioch, a city in modern-day Syria*

Question: Why were guilds needed?

Answer: *To control various industries; to help regulate competition, provide employment, and subsidize towns*

Question: When did feudalism end?

Answer: *Feudalism ended all over Europe at the end of the 14th century.*

Question: How did King Richard (Lion Heart) raise money for England after the Crusades?

Answer: *He created a new official seal. People had to pay to use it on legal documents.*

Renaissance Revolutionaries

Materials
- Renaissance Revolutionaries reproducibles
- markers
- reference materials

Objective

Students will compare Renaissance artists, philosophers, and scientists from different regions.

In this challenging game, students employ prior knowledge and deductive reasoning to identify the geniuses of the Renaissance. This game is played similarly to the popular television game show *What's My Line?*® (a registered trademark of FremantleMedia Operations B.V. Corporation New Zealand Media Centre).

Part 1: Background on the Renaissance

1. Begin by initiating a discussion on the Renaissance (1350–1550) as a transition period between the Medieval Era and the modern world. Explain to students that the word *Renaissance* means *revival* or *rebirth*. Ask: *What important aspects of the Renaissance shaped the world then and now?* Review historical information about that period so students understand its importance.

2. Remind students that during the Renaissance period, achievements in the arts and sciences were combined with deep religious concerns. Ask volunteers if they can think of any other period of history in which inventions, politics, religion, and the arts altered the way people thought about their world. One answer might be the Industrial Revolution.

3. Brainstorm the concept of "right place and right time" as it applies to the Renaissance. Explain that learning and scholarship were direct results of the Crusaders, who brought back a newfound understanding of the world.

4. Encourage further discussions on early inventions such as the printing press, which helped develop literacy and spread new ideas across Europe. Include dialogue on the accumulation of wealth and financial techniques, such as bookkeeping, banking, and credit, which helped the merchant class to prosper.

5. Describe to students the concept of "place" as a critical element for the Renaissance to evolve. For example, the Renaissance began in northern Italy and spread throughout Europe. The Italian cities of Naples, Genoa, and Venice were centers for trade between Europe and the Middle East. Arab scholars had preserved ancient Greek writings in libraries. When Italians traded with the Arabs, new ideas were also exchanged. Without central trading locations, new ideas may not have spread.

Part 2: Let the Games Begin!

1. Give students copies of the **Renaissance Revolutionaries reproducibles (pages 57–58)**. Review the list with the class and discuss in detail one person's significant contributions. Ask students to offer more information about that person.

2. Explain to students that they will do their own research on each Renaissance figure. Direct them to find at least three more facts, including biographical information such as date and place of birth, education, and accomplishments. Tell students that their research notes will be used for a game.

3. Allow time for students to research and review information for their Renaissance Revolutionaries reproducibles. Afterward, allow time for students to share their findings with classmates. Encourage them to take notes.

4. Explain the rules of the game to students as you model how to play. Three students will act as panelists, while another student acts as a Renaissance revolutionary. The object of the game is to stump the three panelists as they try to figure out the revolutionary's name and profession.

   a. Three panelists and one Renaissance revolutionary play four standard rounds. A standard round is a guessing game in which the panel tries to identify the occupation of the Renaissance revolutionary by asking "yes" or "no" questions.

   b. If the answer to the first panelist's question is *no*, the next panelist asks a question.

   c. Panelists have the option of passing on their turn if they are stumped.

   d. Panelists may request a group conference to openly discuss ideas about the occupation or name of the Renaissance revolutionary.

   e. Questions continue until the name and occupation of the Renaissance revolutionary is discovered, or until the end of four rounds.

5. Once you feel comfortable that students understand the rules, model a game by having a volunteer pretend to be a familiar storybook character, such as Cinderella. Ask questions such as: *Are you male? Are you fictional? Did you eat a poison apple? Did you wear glass slippers to a ball?* Explain that each question should provide a clue to the identity of the character.

6. Begin the first round of the game by having the Renaissance revolutionary whisper to you his or her name and occupation. The first panelist should open with a broad question such as: *Are you an artist?* If the answer is *yes,* the panelist continues. A *no* moves the questioning to the next panelist, who might ask: *Do you live in Italy?* Panelists must step down if they don't guess correctly after four rounds. Play continues until each student has a turn as a Renaissance revolutionary or a panelist.

7. After the game, ask students if their research and the game helped them to better understand the people and the world of the Renaissance. Invite them to share their favorite Renaissance artist, scientist, or scholar and give specific reasons for their answers.

Extended Learning

- Explain the term *Renaissance Man* (or *Woman*). Have students search reference materials, newspapers, and the Internet to look for a contemporary person who fits the term.

- Describe the term *polymath* to students (a person who is very learned in a variety of areas) as being the Renaissance ideal. As a class, identify several examples of Renaissance polymaths. Encourage students to explain why certain developments of the Renaissance created a fertile environment for polymaths.

Name _____ Date _____

Renaissance Revolutionaries

Directions: Research more facts about each person and write them on the lines.

Martin Luther (1483–1546)
- Leader of Protestant Reformation
- Criticized Pope for selling indulgences
- Said the *Bible* should be the sole authority on the church
- Translated *Bible* from Latin to German, available to commoners

_____

_____

_____

_____

_____

Nicolo Machiavelli (1469–1527)
- Political and military theorist
- Florentine statesman and patriot
- Wrote *The Art of War, History of Florence*, and *The Prince*
- Said to be the father of modern political science

_____

_____

_____

_____

_____

William Shakespeare (1564–1616)
- One of the greatest dramatists and poets in the English language
- Plays include *Hamlet, Romeo and Juliet*, and *Macbeth*
- Published 154 sonnets
- His plays are still produced today

_____

_____

_____

_____

_____

Nicolaus Copernicus (1473–1543)
- Lawyer, tax collector, doctor, military governor, and astronomer
- Said that Earth turned on its axis and revolved around the sun
- His findings marked the beginning of a revolution in astronomy

_____

_____

_____

_____

_____

Renaissance Revolutionaries

Directions: Research more facts about each person and write them on the lines.

René Descartes (1596–1650)

- Philosopher, scientist, and mathematician
- First to describe the universe in terms of matter and motion
- Wrote *Discourse on Method* and *Principles of Philosophy*
- Said the world was made of two substances: matter and spirit

_____

_____

_____

_____

Galileo Galilei (1564–1642)

- Philosopher, scientist, and mathematician
- Published book about the theories of Ptolemy and Copernicus
- Arrested for heresy
- Developed important improvements to the telescope

_____

_____

_____

_____

Filippo Brunelleschi (1377–1446)

- Father of Renaissance architecture
- Developed ways to make a dome without support or scaffolding
- Developed linear perspective; showed depth on a flat surface
- His book, *Rules of Perspective*, influenced Michelangelo

_____

_____

_____

_____

Gerardus Mercator (1518–1594)

- Leading mapmaker of the 15th century
- First to use longitude and latitude lines on maps
- First to make an accurate map of the British Isles
- His maps and globes helped increase trade and exploration

_____

_____

_____

_____

"Magna Carta" Relay Race

Objective

Students will understand the importance of historical legal practices and their influence on modern democratic ideas.

Materials
• "Magna Carta" True or False reproducible
• 2 flags or banners
• 2 clay or Styrofoam balls, cut in half
• index cards

This invigorating relay race combines physical activity with mental stimulation. Student teams will research the topics and race to be the first to recall the information. This game builds academic skills as well as confidence and peer cooperation. It can be played indoors or outdoors with props, if available.

1. Review with students the concept of true or false statements. For example: *Our school has stables and horses. Is this statement true or false?* (false) *Our school has teachers and students. Is this statement true or false?* (true) Next, ask who has competed in a relay race. Have a volunteer explain how to run a relay race.

2. Tell students that they will be running a relay race. As a twist, they will need to identify if a statement is true or false. The topic will be the Magna Carta. Ask a volunteer to provide a few details about the Magna Carta, such as: *It is a document signed by King John of England in 1215. King John made promises to his barons that he would govern England according to the rule of law.*

3. Ahead of time, make two copies of the **"Magna Carta" True or False reproducible (page 61)**. Allow time for students to work in groups to research the Magna Carta and brainstorm more true or false statements. Have each group write their statements on a sheet of paper. There should be at least one statement for each student.

4. On a table or two separate desks, set up two stations, each with a pencil, the "Magna Carta" True or False reproducible (with additional sheets of students' true/false statements stapled to the back), and a half-ball of clay or Styrofoam to hold the flag.

5. Divide the class into two teams. Have them choose team names that relate to the time period of the Magna Carta. For example, they could be the Knights and the Serfs. Have each team line up at a distance from a station. The first player in each line holds the team flag. Explain that the object of the game is for each player to correctly identify whether a statement is true or false. After the last player is finished, he or she will stick the flag into the holder.

6. Ask three volunteers to model the relay race. To begin, the first player (holding the flag) runs to the table and reads the first statement on the reproducible. He or she must then write *True* or *False* next to the statement and stick the flag into the holder. As soon as a flag is placed, check that the answer is correct. Then the player runs back to his or her team and passes the flag to the next player and play continues.

7. Tell students that players on each team take turns answering questions. Each correct answer earns five points. If a player does not know the correct answer, he or she should run back to consult with team members. Incorrect answers will lose a team ten points. The first team to plant their final flag gets 20 points.

8. Answer any questions and then begin the race. Afterward, add up the points by reading each statement aloud and asking students if the answers are correct. The team with the most points wins. For the next round, make the race more interesting by instructing students to run in different ways. For example, have one student skip, the next run backwards, and the next stop every five steps to do a jumping jack.

9. After the first race, ask students to research the false statements and make them true by correcting the information.

Extended Learning

- Have students access and explore The Knights, Chivalry, and Tournaments Resource Library Web site at: *www.chronique.com*. Here they can find information about knights, weapons, and armor. This site also includes interesting information about the Magna Carta.

- To reinforce the topic of study, play Whose Bag Is This? Fill paper bags with items typical of the time period being studied. Use items like pictures, drawings, or toys to represent things that a person of a particular position or social class may have used. Have the class guess to what type of person the items belong.

"Magna Carta" True or False

1. The Pope insisted that King John sign the Magna Carta.

2. The Magna Carta was signed in 1215.

3. The Magna Carta was signed in the Tower of London.

4. The main goal of the barons was to establish freedom for all Englishmen.

5. The main goal of King John was to regain the support of the barons.

6. Richard the Lion Heart was King John's brother.

7. There were 36 chapters in the Magna Carta.

8. The Magna Carta stated that rule of law is more important than the king's will.

9. The Magna Carta guaranteed that the punishment should fit the crime.

10. The barons did not want to pay heavy taxes to the king.

11. Robert Fitzwalter was the Archbishop of Canterbury.

12. Magna Carta means "The Great Charter."

13. After the Magna Carta was signed, King John honored all of its points.

14. One of the main points in the Magna Carta was that the church was free to appoint an archbishop.

15. The Magna Carta created income tax.

16. Pope Innocent III declared the Magna Carta to be null and void.

17. The Magna Carta forgave the debts of the common man.

18. The final version of the Magna Carta was confirmed with changes in 1216, 1217, and 1225.

Spanish Conquest Mingle

Materials
- Spanish Conquest Mingle Cards reproducible
- scissors
- index cards
- timer

Objective
Students will learn the lasting effects of military conquests during the Middle Ages.

Non-competitive mingling games are often used as icebreakers. Students can relax and have fun in an environment conducive to learning. To play this game, students must recall information but are not required to be in the spotlight. Feel free to use this game with any topic of study.

1. Provide students with some background information about Spanish Conquests: *In 716, Muslim Moors had conquered most of the territory of Spain and Portugal. Christian Spaniards began a long "holy war" or crusade, called* **reconquista**, *to regain the land. With the support of the Pope, at the end of the 12th century, a combined Christian army regained most of the territory they had lost. All that was left of Muslim Spain was Grenada, which fell later in 1492. Spain, as with other European countries during that time, had a small number of wealthy landlords. When Spain captured Moorish regions, the landlords dominated the peasant class by imposing religious, economic, and cultural restraints.*

2. Ask students to define the term *subjugation*. The term relates to words like *conquest, conquer, exploitation,* and *mistrust*. Write these and other related words on the board.

3. Explain that after Spain conquered the Moors, the Spaniards went on a voyage of conquest to the New World. Compare the two peoples, the Moors and the American Indians, and how they were treated by the Spaniards. Suggest that the term *subjugation* also applies to how the Spaniards treated the American Indians.

   (Note that most Spanish attempts at subjugation were only partially successful in the Americas. Native Americans managed to maintain control of many outlying areas. Native groups were also able to blend Christianity within their own traditional beliefs and continued to secretly worship in the old ways.)

4. To give students more background about the Spanish conquests, write the following Worlds Collide timeline on the board. Discuss each item with students and invite them to share their thoughts about each event.

5. Explain that the Spanish empire exploited resources such as gold and silver. They used native populations, often by force, as a class of laborers. Inform students that the Native Americans were also forced to work in fields and mines. Their rights and autonomy were taken.

6. Discuss Spain's involvement in the colonization of the Americas, particularly Chile. Explain that up to the 15th century, tribes occupying northern portions of Chile had been subjugated by the Incas in Peru.

7. Photocopy the **Spanish Conquest Mingle Cards reproducible (page 65)** and cut out the cards. Supplement these game cards by inviting students to work in pairs to research more information about the Spanish Conquests. Have them write questions and answers on separate index cards. If you wish, allow students to preview the information before playing the game. Mix up the cards.

8. Tell students that the goal of this game is to match questions and answers. Half of the cards have questions; the other half have the answers. The goal is for partners to find each other. For example, a student who has the card with the question *Who is King Phillip II?* must look for and find the student with the answer *King of Spain 1556–1598 and great-grandson of Ferdinand and Isabella.*

9. Read the following directions to the class. Ask for four volunteers to model the game. Have students line up facing away from you. Tape two questions and answers to the students' backs. Explain that they may not look at their cards, but others may.
   a. Players begin with a card taped to their back, either a question or an answer.
   b. Players must match questions and answers in the period of time allotted.
   c. At your signal, students mingle around the room reading others' cards. Players may ask "yes" or "no" questions to determine the information on their own card. For example: *Am I a question card? Is my question about the Pope?*
   d. Once students know about their own card, they can search for their match.
   e. When students find their match, they sit down together.
   f. The first three teams to sit down win the game.

10. Answer any questions about the game. Set a timer for five minutes and begin play. Watch for the players who find their matches first and write down their names. Continue to let students find their matches until time is up. Ask students who found matches to read their cards to the class.

11. Then encourage the rest of the class to find their matches. Assist students as needed. If there are incorrect matches, have students discuss why they thought the matches worked. Ask other students to offer reasons why the correct matches make more sense.

Extended Learning

- Based on the knowledge gained through the course of the game, have students summarize their experiences by creating their own newspaper featuring events from Spanish Conquests. They may recreate or embellish events. Encourage them to write rich stories that provide a sense of history, time, and place.

- Invite students to investigate more people and facts about Spanish Conquests or another current topic of study. Suggest that they use the information to make additional game cards to play another mingling game.

What is Feudal Spain?	European country that conquered and dominated the Iberian Peninsula and much of the Americas	**Who is the Pope?**	Principal head of Catholic Church; during the Middle Ages, popes held power equal to kings of countries
What is a "holy war"?	A war in which people of one religious belief fight against those of another belief	**What are the Crusades?**	A "holy war" begun in 1095 by Pope Urban II to fight against Muslims for faith and Jerusalem
Who is King Phillip II?	King of Spain 1556–1598 and great-grandson of Ferdinand and Isabella	**What is Chile?**	Modern name of South American country conquered by Spanish Conquistadors
Who is Francisco Pizzaro?	Spanish conquistador who defeated the Inca Empire	**Who are the Inca?**	Native people who ruled a kingdom in South America; Spanish armies destroyed them in 50 years
What is religious intolerance?	Unwillingness to grant equal freedom or expression in religious matters	**What did the Conquistadors want?**	Gold, silver, slaves, exotic animals
What is Imperialism?	To impose a government's political system, religion, culture, or economics on another nation	**What are Cordoba and Baghdad?**	Two Moorish cities known for scholarship where new ideas were born

CHAPTER 4

World Cultures

Pin the House on the Map

Materials
- Dwellings and Structures Picture Cards reproducibles
- picture of ancient dwelling, such as the Anasazi ruins of Canyon de Chelly
- wall map of the world
- scissors
- crayons or markers
- double-sided tape
- timer

Objective

Students will recognize how environment influences human dwellings.

Using the familiar format of a simple game such as Pin the Tail on the Donkey is an excellent way to teach more complex topics. This game helps students recognize relationships between people, places, and environments, but it may also be used with any topic of study.

1. Tell students that throughout history people have learned to adapt to their surroundings. Show a picture of an ancient dwelling, such as the Anasazi ruins of Canyon de Chelly. Ask students to describe the dwelling. Write their responses on the board. Initiate a discussion about who the builders were, why they built their homes in caves, and what materials they used.

2. Point out that although the dwelling is from a specific time period, later groups who moved into the same region brought their own skills, knowledge, and standards. Ask students who some of these people might have been. Answers might include: *Pueblo Indians (Zuni, Hopi, and so on) and later, nomadic groups such as the Navaho (Dine)*.

3. Give students a copy of the **Dwellings and Structures Picture Cards reproducibles (pages 68–69)**. Have them review the pictures and discuss why the houses belong to certain geographic locations and continents. For example, point out the Masaai House of East Africa. The homes are made of cow dung and dried grass. Ask students: *Why do you think the builders chose these materials?* Answers might include: *There were few materials in the region for people to make homes. Dried cow dung acts like mud and makes secure, warm homes.*

4. Discuss some important geographic and weather conditions, such as freezing wind, which might have influenced builders. Point out the igloo on the reproducible and discuss how people survive in frigid regions of the world. Then have students color and cut out the picture cards on the reproducibles.

5. Ask students if they have ever played Pin the Tail on the Donkey. Ask for a student volunteer to explain the game. Then ask another student to model how to play the game. Give the student three game cards with double-sided tape on the back. In one minute, challenge the student to stick as many picture cards as he or she can to the correct places on a world wall map. Review the placements with the class.

6. Answer any questions about the game and begin play. The player with the most correct placements in one minute wins.

7. After the game, invite students to explore the characteristics of each location on the map where a house was placed. Discuss why each home works best in each environment. Then continue your discussion about different kinds of homes used in the United States (e.g., houses, apartments, condos, trailer homes, houses on stilts along the coast where flooding may occur, and so on).

Extended Learning
Have students research different regions' flora and fauna and play the game using pictures of plants or animals.

Dwellings and Structures Picture Cards

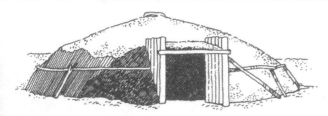

**North America:
Plains Earth Lodge, Nebraska**

**North America:
Hogan of the Navaho (Dine)**

North America: Tipi of the Oglala Indians

North America: Igloo in Alaska

Africa: Maasai House of East Africa

Africa: Zulu Hut in South Africa

Africa: Ashanti River Hut in Ghana

Africa: Bantu Dwelling in South Africa

Europe: Farm Dwelling in Finland

Europe: Sod House in Ireland

Dwellings and Structures Picture Cards

Europe: Palace Hall in Spain

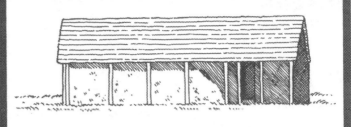

Europe: Viking House in Germany

Europe: Greek Temple in Greece

South America: Inca Dwelling in Peru

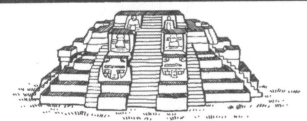

South America: Mayan
Temple in Guatemala

South America: Aztec Dwelling in Mexico

Asia: Yurt Dwelling in Mongolia

Asia: Post House at Nong
Chae Sao in Thailand

Asia: Horyu-ji Temple in Japan

Australia: Aboriginal Dwelling

Samurai Says!

Materials
- Japanese Feudal Society reproducibles
- index cards
- paper lunch bag
- sticky nametags
- black marker

Objective

Students will identify the lifestyle of citizens from Ancient Japan.

Familiar childhood games such as Simon Says can motivate students of all ages. Elements of surprise and role play foster student engagement while developing listening skills and cooperation. In this game, students gain an understanding of the tiers of feudal Japanese society by researching the topic and incorporating the information into the game. Play this game inside or outside.

1. Ask students to raise their hands if they have ever played Simon Says. Ask a volunteer to explain how the game is played. Play a quick round with students at their desks. Use commands such as: *Raise your right hand. Tap your right foot. Pat your head.* Give the commands quickly to make it more fun. Afterward, explain that they will be playing a similar game called Samurai Says!

2. Pass out copies of the **Japanese Feudal Society reproducibles (pages 72–73)** to students. Write the list of titles on the board. Discuss the members of Japanese feudal society. Ask for additional examples such as acolyte, Buddhist monk, Shinto priest, pilgrim, and slave. Add student suggestions to the list on the board.

3. Discuss the classes of feudal Japan. Mention that the arts and literature were highly respected means of entertainment and communication. Discuss gender roles and explain that some women from the higher classes were educated and wrote poetry, diaries, and myths. Two of these works include *The Tale of Genji* and *The Pillow Book*. Ask students: *Would you like to live in Japanese feudal society? If so, who would you want to be? Why? What were the difficulties for each societal level?*

4. Ask volunteers to write the Japanese society classes and titles from the board on index cards, one for each student in the class. For example: *First Level: Noble* or *Sixth Level: Basket Maker.* Make sure the selections reflect feudal Japanese society. For example, there should be one shogun, emperor, and empress, but multiple farmers, merchants, and outcasts. Collect the index cards and place them in a bag.

5. Invite each student to draw one card from the bag and then write the social class and role on a sticky nametag. Students should wear their nametags in easy view of the "Samurai" caller.

6. Read the following directions to the class and encourage students to practice getting into character. Played like Simon Says, the object of the game is for the Samurai caller to catch the players off guard.

    a. A Samurai caller may command an entire social class or a specific title. Commands should be simple, such as: *Jump on one foot. Take a step forward. Take a step back.*

    b. Players must listen for their class and title and respond when the caller gives them a command starting with *Samurai says!* If they do not respond, they are out of the game.

    c. Players who respond to the wrong title or to a command that does not begin with *Samurai says!* are out of the game.

    d. The first player to cross the line where the caller is standing wins and becomes the next Samurai caller.

7. Model a round for the class by acting as the Samurai caller. Stand a distance away from the players and have players stand in a line facing you. Use commands such as: *Samurai says, beggars take one step forward.* If you simply say: *Beggars, take one step forward*, players should not respond. Give commands quickly to try to trick the players.

8. Make sure students understand the rules of the game and then choose one student to be the first Samurai caller. Monitor the game to make sure students respond correctly to the commands.

9. After the first round, increase the challenge by calling on different characters to act out or tell you their duties or "role" in Japanese feudal society. Or, ask them to line up in order of their level in society.

10. After the game, invite students to interact with each other for a few minutes in character. Or have them gather into groups to act out various scenarios that reflect feudal Japan.

Extended Learning

- Arrange for a follow-up activity such as a trip to a museum that is exhibiting feudal Japanese artwork and culture.

- Have for the class watch the PBS documentary *Japan: Memoirs of a Secret Empire.*

Japanese Feudal Society

First Level: Imperial Family, Empress, Nobles, Political Advisors, Courtesans

The emperor was at the top of the social ladder in Japanese society but had limited power. The royal society included no more than 140 families. Their finances and lives were tightly scrutizined and controlled.

Second Level: Shogun

The shogun was the most powerful position and military leader in Japan. He had absolute power and control, even over the emperor.

Third Level: Daimyos, Feudal Lords

The country was divided into 250 clan dominions. To qualify for daimyo status, the feudal lord had to control enough land to produce rice to feed 10,000 men in one year.

Fourth Level: Samurai Warriors (Elite), Masterless Samurai (Ronin), Samurai Women

Samurai served their lord daimyos, even unto death. Samurai were given special freedoms without fear of reprisal from authorities.

Japanese Feudal Society

Fifth Level: Farmers

The bulk of the population included villagers who worked the land. Their livelihood depended upon the harvest.

Sixth Level: Craftsmen–Swordsmiths, Printmakers, Poets, Flower Artists (Ikibani), Calligraphers, Basket Makers, Weavers

These citizens lived in towns and did not grow their own food products. Swordsmiths were considered the highest level of this group.

Seventh Level: Merchants–Tea and Sake Sellers, Innkeepers, Booksellers, Street Vendors

Although they were low on the social ladder, merchants controlled much of the financial power.

Eighth Level: Outcasts

This group included beggars and anyone considered unclean. The outcast group included butchers and tanners who handled dead animals.

The Islamic Golden Age: Baseball

Materials
- Islamic Math and Science reproducible
- Islamic Medicine and Education reproducible
- 4 plastic rings
- 4 plastic stakes (or chalk)
- 4 plastic rings
- 4 beanbags

Objective
Students will understand the contributions made by the Islamic culture of the Middle Ages.

The game *Quoits* (similar to horseshoes) dates back hundreds of years or more. Students will play a game that combines Quoits with a twist on American baseball. This game is a stimilating way for students to use motor skills and hand–eye coordination while reviewing any topic of study.

1. Explain to students that Quoits is an ancient game played similarly to horseshoes. Have a volunteer explain the goal of horseshoes. Quoits is similar in some ways, but rather than trying to hit one target, a player may choose one of four. Note that this version of the game includes elements of baseball, too.

2. Have a student write the numbers *1–10* on the board. Point out that these numbers are a modern form of the Arabic number system. Explain that Muslim scholars of the Middle Ages were devoted to knowledge, and they brought about many important advances in math, science, medicine, and education. Give students copies of the **Islamic Math and Science** and **Islamic Medicine and Education reproducibles (pages 76–77)**. Allow students time to review the information.

3. Ahead of time, make a list of questions, by category, based on the information provided on the reproducibles. Share a couple of your questions with the class and then invite them to write similar types of questions for the game, at least two for each category: math, science, medicine, and education.

4. Outside, create a playing field by placing four stakes in a square pattern in the ground, with stakes about three feet apart in the shape of a baseball diamond. Or, draw chalk squares on the ground as "bases." Place a beanbag at each base. Label each stake or square *Math, Science, Medicine,* or *Education.*

5. Explain to students that each base stands for a category of questions: math, science, medicine, or education. Players will try to toss a ring over a stake (or into a chalk square). When a player "catches" a stake, he or she gets the opportunity to answer a question in that category. A "miss" means the turn goes to a player on the other team. (You will ask the questions, or you may invite a volunteer to ask them.)

6. Players move ahead just like in baseball. A player gets three tries to think of the correct answer, and then he or she is "out." Each inning has three outs. If the player answers correctly, he or she moves to first base, and the next "batter" is up. Players advance one base after each correct answer. When a player crosses home plate, the team scores one run. The team with the most runs after nine innings wins the game.

7. Model the game by taking a turn at bat. Throw the ring and answer the question to move to first base, and then move on to second base. Answer any questions to make sure students understand the rules of the game. Then divide the class into two teams and begin the game.

8. After the game, ask students to select one achievement from the reproducibles that they consider a "home run" for the world. Encourage them to give reasons to support their choices.

Extended Learning

Ask students to swap out categories for the game. For example, they can create a selection of questions on the contributions of Islamic artists and writers of the Middle Ages.

Islamic Math and Science

Math

- We use a system of Arabic numbers based on units of tens, with place values and a zero. These numbers replaced the Roman system.

- Muslim mathematicians introduced the use of fractions and decimal fractions.

- Al-Khwarizmi is called the "Father of Algebra." His work was one of the first to include proofs. It was based on information from Greeks, Alexandrians, and Hindus. The term *algebra* comes from the Arabic word *al-jabr*, meaning "return of balance."

- Al-Tusi is called the "Father of Trigonometry." This branch of mathematics studies plane and spherical triangles. The idea began with the Greeks and was developed by Al-Tusi.

- Muslim scholars translated and preserved the works of the Greeks, including Euclid's work on geometry.

- Arabic words that are now mathematical terms include *algebra* and *algorithm*.

Science

- Ibn Haiyan is known for writing many books on chemistry and alchemy. He developed methods to show the same result when an experiment was repeated.

- Al-Farghani was an astronomer. His books were translated into Latin and widely read in Europe. He believed that the sun was the center of a system of planets.

- Al-Sufi was the first to describe the Andromeda galaxy. This was the first record of a galaxy outside of our own.

- Al-Zarqali made a kind of astrolabe that measured the motion of the stars. His work was translated into many languages, and his books were studied in Europe.

- Ibn Sahl developed the first accurate theory of refraction of light.

- Arabic words that are now scientific terms include *chemistry*, *almanac*, *alcohol*, and *elixir*.

Islamic Medicine and Education

Medicine

- Al-Rhazi discovered the origin of smallpox, which led to the discovery of the immune system. He also developed treatments for chickenpox and measles.

- Ibn Sina wrote an encyclopedia of medicine. It included information on hygiene, anatomy, and many illnesses and cures. He was the first to note the way that tuberculosis spread and to examine the nature of contagious diseases.

- Al-Zahravi is called the "Father of Surgery." He perfected several operations, developed surgical tools, and was the first to use silk thread for stitching wounds.

- The Arab world established the first drugstores. Registered pharmacists had to pass formal examinations to run them.

- A hospital was established in every major Muslim city. The hospital in Cairo had more than 8,000 beds.

- Arabic words that are now medical terms include *aorta, pancreas, colon,* and *cornea.*

Education

- The first colleges were built in the Muslim world several hundred years before European colleges. The mosque of Al-Azhar became a university in the 10th century. Classes were taught in science, religion, law, and language.

- In the House of Wisdom, Baghdad, scholars translated works of the Greeks, Egyptians, and others into Arabic. Their work preserved much classical knowledge.

- The medical school at the University of Jundishapur was established in the 9th century. It taught medical practices from Arab countries, Greece, China, and India.

- In the 9th century, the library of Cordoba contained more than 500,000 volumes.

- Observatories to study the planets were built in major cities such as Baghdad, Toledo, Samarkand, and Istanbul.

- After Baghdad fell to the Mongols in 1258, schools and other institutions were burned. All books in the House of Wisdom were destroyed.

CHAPTER 5

Government and Citizenship

United Nations Student Feud

Objective
Students will understand how having geographical awareness is a significant tool in interpreting the present and planning for the future.

Materials
- construction paper
- black markers
- masking tape

Television game shows can easily be adapted to the classroom. This game is based on the popular game show *Family Feud*® (a registered trademark of FremantleMedia Operations B.V. Corporation by change of name Netherlands Media Centre) and is designed to provide students with an understanding of the facts, details, and cultural issues involved with the United Nations. During play, students support each other and receive feedback while challenging themselves and their teammates.

1. Initiate a discussion with students about the inner workings, history, and contemporary issues of the United Nations. Review the historical beginnings of the United Nations, articles, member states, languages, location of the main headquarters, and the color and significance of the flag. All of this information is available at the United Nations Web site: *www.un.org*.

2. Choose six to ten questions about the United Nations that have multiple answers and write them on the board. For example: *Which nations are permanent members of the United Nations Security Council?* Answer: *China, France, Russian Federation, United Kingdom,* and *United States.* Review the questions and answers with students. Then erase the answers from the board.

3. To play the game, students must first set up the survey. Have students write the questions from the board on a sheet of paper and then write as many answers as they can for each question. Collect students' papers and tally the answers. For example: *What are the official languages of the UN?* There are six correct answers. The order in which they were answered, based on a survey of 25 students, might be: *English (11), Spanish (6), French (4), Russian (2), Chinese (1),* and *Arabic (1).* Make a note of the top five answers only. The number of students who gave the answer is the point value of the answer. For example, the answer *English* is worth 11 points.

4. Ask volunteers to use black marker to write each question on a piece of construction paper. Have them write out answers *1, 2, 3, 4,* and *5.* Tape each sheet to the wall, with the questions and their answers according to point value underneath and in order. Tape a sheet of paper on top to cover the question and answers.

5. Explain to students that they will be playing the United Nations Student Feud game, which is based on the TV game show *Family Feud®*. Then explain the following rules. The object of the game is to earn points by determining the most popular answers in the survey. Two teams will compete, just like the families on the game show.

   a. The host reads a survey question to the first team.

   b. The first player tries to guess the most popular answer in the survey. An answer is correct if it is one of the concealed answers on the board.

   c. If the first player gives an answer that appears on the board in any position, award his or her team the point value for that answer.

   d. The next player on the team gives another answer to the question. Each player on the team gets a chance to give one answer.

   e. Teammates may not confer with each other, and whispering or shouting answers is not allowed.

   f. At the end of the round, award the team the combined point value for each correct answer.

   g. The next team then gets a chance to play.

6. Model one question with the class, using invented survey results. Divide the class into teams of five students each. Place five chairs in two lines opposite each other and post the questions and answers between the two teams.

7. Note that the goal of playing this game is to get the top answer to as many questions as possible. Once you feel students understand the game, have the first two teams take their places. Ask for two volunteers, one to add up points for each team and another to lift the cover sheets off of the questions and answers as they are given. Have the "answer volunteer" check the answers before the game so he or she knows where they are. Remind students that they cannot confer with each other if they do not know an answer.

8. Begin play by reading the question to the first player. Before the volunteer reveals if the answer receives points, say: *Survey says. . . .* Instruct the volunteer to lift the paper off of the correct answer. Instruct the other volunteer to keep track of the points earned. Move on to the next player. Continue the round until all the correct answers are given or two incorrect answers are given. If two incorrect answers are given, play moves to the next team. The team with the most points accumulated wins the game.

9. After the game, ask students to offer ways to make the game more difficult or interesting.

Extended Learning

Try adapting other game shows to the classroom. For example, a game played similarly to To Tell the Truth® (a registered trademark of FremantleMedia Operations B.V.) could be fun and informative. Choose three students to form a panel and pretend that they are a political or historical figure, such as the president of the United States. The class gets to ask questions of each panelist and decide which of the three is the real U.S. president.

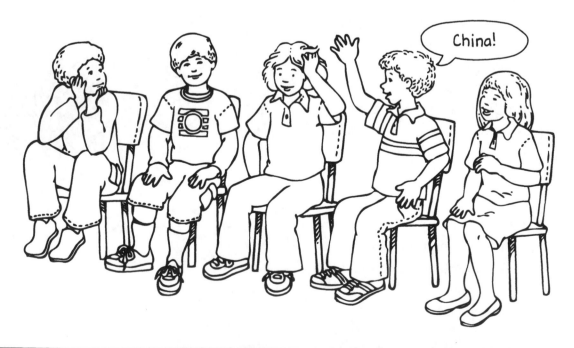

"Checks and Balances" Hot Potato

Objectives

Students will identify the three branches of the U.S. government. Students will understand that the structure of the U.S. government is based on the separation and balance of powers.

Materials
- Checks and Balances reproducible
- beanbag
- music CDs or cassettes
- CD or cassette player

This game makes learning fun by adding an element of suspense to a review session. It can be used for any topic of study and played indoors or outdoors in small or large groups. Because students stand and pass around the "potato," there is a physical element that helps kinesthetic learners as well.

1. Ask students to name some of their favorite party games from early childhood. Ask if any students have played Hot Potato. Explain that they will be playing a game similar to Hot Potato to review the topic of checks and balances in the U.S. government.

2. Explain that the U.S. government is made up of three branches. Ask volunteers to name them. *(legislative branch, executive branch, judicial branch)* Initiate a discussion about what is meant by *separation of powers*. Allow students to research the topic. Give them a copy of the **Checks and Balances reproducible (page 83)** to review.

3. Play this game in one large group or separate the class into two teams. Tell students to form a circle with about one foot of space between players. Then give a beanbag to the first student. When you give the signal (turn on the music), the player will treat the beanbag like a hot potato and pass it quickly to the next player, and so on, around the circle. Ask the first few players in the circle to model how this is done on your signal.

4. Tell students that when the music stops, the person holding the beanbag will answer a question based on information from the Checks and Balances reproducible. You may choose to ask the questions or select a volunteer to ask the questions.

5. Answer any questions about the game. When students are ready, start the music and have them start passing the "hot potato." Stop the music after 30–40 seconds.

6. The student holding the hot potato must step into the center of the circle. Ask him or her a question based on information from the reproducible. If someone drops the hot potato, the last person to hold it must answer a question. If the student answers correctly, he or she is safe and remains in the game. An incorrect response means the student is out.

7. If the student chooses, he or she can challenge another student to answer. If the challenged student answers correctly, the challenger is out. If the challenged player does not give the correct answer, he or she is out. The game is over when only one person is left— the winner!

8. After the game, allow time for students to talk more about the checks and balances structure of the U.S. government. Ask them why these checks and balances are important in forming a democracy.

Extended Learning

- Adapt this activity into a Hot Potato vocabulary game. When the music stops, ask the player holding the hot potato to define a term such as *congress, representative, senator, Constitution, law, override, ratify, rider, veto,* or *pocket veto.*

- Initiate a discussion with students about how a free press adds to the system of checks and balances. Ask students to research examples of how the free press has recently had an impact on the government.

- Invite students to explore the Branches of the Government section on the Truman Library Web site: *www.trumanlibrary.org/ whistlestop/teacher_lessons/3branches/0.htm.*

Checks and Balances

The Founding Fathers of the United States recognized the need to clearly divide power among the three branches of government. Because of this, the legislative, executive, and judicial branches must cooperate with each other. This guarantees that no one branch is more powerful than the others and reduces the risk that one branch can abuse its power.

Legislative Branch

This branch, or Congress, is made up of the House of Representatives and the Senate. Congress makes laws. Voters elect members of Congress.

Checks Executive Branch

- May override a presidential veto
- May impeach the president
- Confirms presidential appointments
- Authorizes federal funds for legislation
- Approves treaties
- Approves federal budget
- May declare war

Checks Judicial Branch

- May impeach judges
- Must confirm federal judges
- Sets number of judges

Executive Branch

This branch is led by the president, who carries out U.S. laws. Voters elect the president through a system using the Electoral College.

Checks Legislative Branch

- Proposes legislation
- May veto or sign legislation
- May make treaties
- May call special sessions of Congress

Checks Judicial Branch

- Appoints federal judges
- Enforces court decisions
- Nominates Supreme Court justices
- May grant pardons or reprieves or commute sentences

Judicial Branch

This branch is made up of the Supreme Court and lower courts. It interprets laws. Justices are appointed for life and confirmed by Congress.

Checks Executive Branch

- Reviews executive acts
- May declare executive orders unconstitutional

Checks Legislative Branch

- Reviews congressional laws
- May declare laws unconstitutional

Renewable Resources Recall

Objective

Students will understand the difference between renewable and non-renewable resources.

The "give and take" of information between peers actively engages students' brains in learning. Renewable Resources Recall is played similarly to the television game show *Are You Smarter Than a Fifth Grader?*® (a registered trademark of JMBP, Inc.). During the game, students are allowed a variety of options to find the answers to questions.

1. Ask students to name the benefits of working together in study groups. Point out that sometimes it is helpful to discuss answers. Think of a question such as: *What is the definition of **acidity**? What team won the last Stanley Cup in hockey?* Choose a random student to answer. He or she most likely will not know the answer at first. Then allow the student to confer with classmates until they have determined the answer together.

2. Introduce the topic of renewable resources. Discuss with the class the hidden costs of practices associated with non-renewewable resources, such as dangerous working conditions, transportation costs, pollution, waste, and loss of natural habitats. Then ask students what they know about renewable natural resources, such as solar energy and wind power.

3. Tell students they will play a game based on the television show *Are You Smarter Than a Fifth Grader?*® To prepare for the game, pass out copies of the **Renewable Resources Fact Sheet reproducibles (pages 86–87)**. Allow time for students to study the information. Choose a panel of five student "experts." Assign each expert one section to study and master, doing additional research as needed.

4. Explain that in this game, you will ask players a question based on the information on the reproducible. Students will have three options for answering: answer on their own, consult an expert, or take a class vote.
   a. If players are certain about the answer, they can answer right away. If the answer is correct, players earn three points.
   b. If players are uncertain about the answer, they can ask for help from a student expert. A correct answer with the help of an expert earns two points.

c. If players are not confident about their own or an expert's answer, they can ask for a vote from the classroom "audience." A correct answer with classroom participation earns one point.

5. Ask two volunteers to help model a round of play. One will be the expert, and the other will try to answer the question.

6. Make sure students understand the rules of the game before beginning. After a few rounds of play, have players switch roles with the experts. Give everyone the opportunity to participate in both the expert and player roles.

7. After the game, ask students which role they preferred—the giver or receiver of information—and why.

Extended Learning

- Use the information from the reproducible to play a simple ball-tossing game. Have students stand in circle. Call out an energy source and toss a ball to a student. The student who catches the ball must answer *renewable* or *non-renewable*, and then toss the ball to another student who will answer the next question.

- Another fun game you can play with students is musical chairs. Instead of playing music, read a list of resources as students walk around a group of chairs (one less than the number of students). Instruct students to sit down when they hear you read the name of a non-renewable resource. The student without a chair is out of the game. Remove one chair and continue.

Renewable Resources Fact Sheet

Biomass

- The most common form of biomass is wood.

- Biomass is organic material made from plants and animals.

- Energy in sunlight is stored as chemical energy in plants.

- Some examples of biomass fuels are wood, crops, manure, and some garbage.

- When burned, the chemical energy in biomass is released as heat.

- Methane gas is the main ingredient of natural gas.

- Crops like corn and sugar cane can be fermented to produce the fuel *ethanol*.

- Garbage is also called "municipal solid waste."

- Food scraps, lawn clippings, and leaves are all examples of biomass trash.

- Biodiesel is safe, is biodegradable, and reduces emissions of most air pollutants.

- Biodiesel fuel can be produced from food products like vegetable oils and fats.

- Ethanol is an alcohol fuel made from the sugars found in grains, such as corn, sorghum, and wheat, as well as potato skins, rice, sugar cane, sugar beets, and yard clippings.

Water

- The ocean provides tidal and wave energy resources.

- There are currently two commercial-sized tidal energy stations. One is in La Rance, France; the other is in Nova Scotia, Canada.

- The world's highest tides are in the Bay of Fundy, Canada.

- Tidal turbines are located anywhere there is strong tidal flow.

- Waves are caused by wind blowing over the ocean's surface.

- One way to use wave energy is to direct waves into a narrow channel.

- Hydropower is most often used to generate electricity.

- In a hydropower system, water may be stored in reservoirs created by dams.

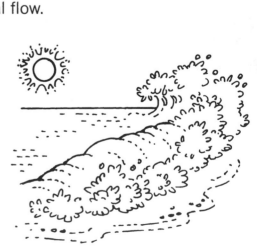

Renewable Resources Fact Sheet

Geothermal

- Geothermal energy comes from heat sources within the earth.

- There are more than 40 power plants in the U.S. producing electricity from geothermal energy.

- Most geothermal power plants in the U.S. are located in California and Nevada.

- Geothermal energy may be used as a heat source in greenhouses.

- The capital of Iceland, Reykjavik, is heated mostly by geothermal energy.

- Geothermal energy produces little if any air pollution.

Wind

- Wind is air in motion.

- Wind is caused by uneven heating of the earth's surface by the sun.

- Wind energy is used mainly to generate electricity.

- Ancient cultures built windmills to grind wheat and other grains.

- A standard horizontal wind machine is 20 stories tall.

- Wind power plants are called "wind farms."

- Wind energy produces no air or water pollution.

- Wind farms are located along open plains, shorelines, or mountain gaps.

Solar

- Solar energy is the solar radiation that reaches the earth.

- Solar energy requires a large area to collect it at a useful rate.

- Solar energy is used for heating water, drying agricultural products, and generating electricity.

- Sunlight is converted into electricity through a photovoltaic cell, or solar cell.

- Cloudy conditions and fog can lessen the effectiveness of solar cells.

- A solar cooker can be made from aluminum foil and a cardboard box.

Credit and Debit Tangle

Objective

Students will learn the vocabulary needed to study a unit on credit and debit.

Studies show that students who participate in brisk physical activity often have higher grades than students who are less active. Invite students to play a physical matching game based on the game *Twister®* (a registered trademark of Hasbro, Inc.). They will use their bodies to physically connect and match terms and definitions. The game may be modified for English language learners or students with special needs. It can also be used with other topics of study.

1. Allow students to play a game of Twister® in class, or model how to play it with a couple of student volunteers. Point out that Twister® is a game of balance.

2. Introduce the topic of credit and debit and tell students that they will play a game similar to Twister® to help them learn more about credit and debit. Students will need to bend, twist, and balance to match and "connect" vocabulary words with their definitions.

3. Give students a copy of the **Credit and Debit Vocabulary reproducible (page 90)** to study. Ensure comprehension by reviewing the definitions with the class.

4. Before playing the game, create the game board labels by cutting ten six-inch circles from red poster board and ten six-inch circles from green poster board. Choose ten vocabulary words from the reproducible. Write the words on the red circles and their definitions on the green circles. Stick Velcro tabs in random spots on a rug or towel to use as a game board. Stick Velcro tabs on the back of the colored circles and attach the circles to the tabs on the game board.

5. On one set of index cards, write the vocabulary words and definitions and place them in a paper bag labeled *Vocabulary Words*. On another set of index cards, write the phrases *left hand, right hand, left foot,* and *right foot*. Make multiple sets and place them in a paper bag labeled *Body Parts.*

6. Ask three volunteers to model the game. Players start by standing on the edges of the board. The referee draws one card from the vocabulary bag and two cards from the body-part bag. For example, the referee might draw *capital, left foot,* and *right hand.*

The first player must put his or her left foot on the red circle that says *capital* and right hand on the green circle that contains the definition of *capital*. The referee continues to draw card combinations while players do their best to take positions without losing their balance and falling over.

7. If players fall, use a body part other than hands or feet, or do not match the word to the correct definition, they are out of the game. The winner is the last player standing.

8. Make sure students understand the rules before playing the game. Invite the class into groups of four and have them rotate play. Or, invite each winner to take on the next group of challengers.

9. After everyone has had a chance to play, review the vocabulary words on the reproducible. Invite students to give real-life examples of each term. As a class, create a new game board with other vocabulary words on the list to play the game again.

Credit and Debit Vocabulary

Bank: Financial institution that holds customers' money and makes loans

Barter: Exchange of goods and services for other goods and services

Capital: Wealth as money or property

Consumer: Someone who buys or uses goods and services

Credit: An amount of money owed to or posted to an account

Debit: Debts; expenses against an account

Economics: Study of the production, distribution, and consumption of goods and services

Entrepreneur: Someone who develops and finances a business for profit

Goods: Merchandise for sale or use

Human Resources: People who work for a business or organization

Producer: Person or company that produces goods and services for trade or sale

Resource: Reserve or supply of something

Scarcity: Lack of something

Service: Work done by someone for someone else in exchange for payment

Immigration Bouquets

Objectives

Students will learn of the contributions of immigrants to America. Students will recognize their own global connections.

The use of colorful balloons not only adds novelty and fun to this game, but also symbolizes the vast number of ethnic groups who contributed to the building of our nation. In this game, students will study immigration waves in the United States and gain a better sense of the diversity of this country.

1. Give students some background on immigration to the United States: *The United States is a nation of immigrants. As early as the 1600s, many people immigrated to this land from England to establish colonies. By the 1800s, people left their homes in northern Europe and Asia bound for a new life in America. Immigrants have come from such countries as Ireland, Germany, Scandinavia, and China. Later groups came from Central and South America.*

2. Invite volunteers to discuss their family tree. Ask students: *Why do you think people immigrated to the United States? If you lived in some other place, would you immigrate to the United States today?* Expand the discussion to include some of the benefits of living in the United States and what students feel their responsibilities are as U.S. citizens. Write their ideas on the board.

3. Ask students to think about some famous immigrants in science, medicine, politics, sports, the arts, and business, such as Albert Einstein, Dr. David Ho, Bela Lugosi, Levi Strauss, Sidney Poitier, Zubin Mehta, Mario Andretti, and John Muir. Ask: *How do you think immigrants have had an impact on your life?*

4. Divide the class into teams of five to six students. Encourage teams to brainstorm individuals they would like

to research. Give students a copy of the **Liberty Cards reproducible (page 94)**. Explain that each completed card should include:
- the name of the person being profiled
- where and when the person was born
- the year the person arrived in the United States
- his or her contribution to American society
- one or more interesting facts about the person's life

5. Share the following game directions with the class and copy the Rewards Chart (below) on the board. The object of the game is for each team to make a balloon bouquet that represents as many colors as possible to collect points.
   - Each team may create up to ten liberty cards.
   - Liberty cards may win points in one or more of the four categories. Each category is awarded a different-colored balloon and has a different point value.
   - Each completed liberty card is awarded one or more balloons, according to the Rewards Chart. For example: *Arnold Schwarzenegger* would be a contemporary figure who contributed in art and politics. This would earn one yellow balloon and one blue balloon for a total of five points.
   - Teams must have at least one balloon of each color for any points to count.
   - The team with the most points wins the game.

Rewards Chart

Category	Rewards	Points
Historical figure	Red balloon	1 point
Contemporary figure	Yellow balloon	2 points
Fun fact	Green balloon	2 points
Contributed in more than one area	Blue balloon	3 points

6. Model completing a sample liberty card on the board, using the following information about Sergey Brin. Point out that extra points can be earned for interesting facts or by profiling a person who made contributions in more than one area.

7. Ask students if they have any questions about the game. Once students feel comfortable with how to play, have them begin their research and complete their liberty cards. Allow class time for research or let students complete the cards as a homework assignment.

8. Invite groups to present their liberty cards to the class. Award each group balloons as designated by the Rewards Chart. Distribute hole punches and lengths of string so students can tie each card to its balloon or cluster of balloons. Tally how many points each group has earned.

9. When the game is finished, instruct students to gather all of their balloons in one spot. Ask them what they think the balloons represent. Guide students to see that the balloons represent all the people from other lands that have helped to make the United States a melting pot of dreams and ideas. Remind students that people like this make America a great nation.

Liberty Card
Name: Sergey Brin
Born: 1973 in Moscow, Russia
Arrived in U.S.: 1979
Contributions: Co-founded the Internet search engine Google
Interesting Facts: In 2007, he was first on the PC Magazine list of the 50 most important people on the Web.

Liberty Cards

Directions: Fill out the cards by researching notable immigrants to the United States. Then see how many balloons and points you can collect!

Liberty Card

Name: _____

Born: _____

Arrived in U.S.: _____

Contributions: _____

_____

Interesting Facts: _____

_____

Liberty Card

Name: _____

Born: _____

Arrived in U.S.: _____

Contributions: _____

_____

Interesting Facts: _____

_____

Answer Key

1. False

Correct answer: The barons insisted that King John sign the Magna Carta.

2. True

3. False

Correct answer: The Magna Carta was signed at a meadow at Runnymede.

4. False

Correct answer: The main goal of the barons was to correct abuses against themselves.

5. True

6. True

7. False

Correct answer: There were 63 chapters in the Magna Carta

8. True

9. True

10. True

11. False

Correct answer: The leader of the rebel barons was the Archbishop of Canterbury.

12. True

13. False

Correct answer: King John claimed he was forced to sign the Magna Carta.

14. False

Correct answer: The church had no power over the king.

15. False

Correct answer: The Magna Carta limited the tax that the king could collect.

16. True

17. False

Correct answer: The Magna Carta protected widows from the king and from creditors.

18. True

References

About.com: American History. (n.d.). *Industrial Revolution inventors*. Retrieved May 14, 2007, from http://americanhistory.about.com/library/charts/blchartindrev.htm.

Agatucci, C. (1999). *Cultures and literatures of Asia: Japan timeline 1: Early Japan (to CE 1168)*. Retrieved April 18, 2007, from Central Oregon Community College, Humanities 210 Web site: http://web.cocc.edu/cagatucci/classes/hum210/tml/JapanTML/japanTML.htm.

Ambrose, S. A. (1996). *Undaunted courage: Meriwether Lewis, Thomas Jefferson, and the opening of the American West*. New York, NY: Touchstone Books, Simon & Schuster.

Barrett, T. (1995). *Growing up in Colonial America*. Brookfield, CT: The Millbrook Press, Inc.

Beyers, J. (1998). The biology of human play. *Child Development, 69*(3), 599–600.

Blanch, G., & Stathis R. (2004). *Leaders who changed the world*. Brea, CA: Ballard & Tighe Publishers.

The British Library. (n.d.). *Treasures in full: Magna Carta*. Retrieved April 27, 2007, from http://www.bl.uk/treasures/magnacarta/magna.html.

Cosman, M. P. (1996). *Medieval workbook*. New York, NY: Checkmark Books.

Dickson, A. J. (Ed.). (1989). *Covered wagon days: A journey across the plain in the sixties, and pioneer days in the Northwest. From the private journals of Albert Jerome Dickson*. Lincoln, NE: University of Nebraska.

Encyclopedia Britannica. (n.d.). *Chile*. Retrieved April 6, 2007, from http://www.britannica.com/eb/article-25248.

Energy Information Administration (n.d.). *Energy kid's page*. Retrieved May 1, 2007, from http://www.eia.doe.gov/kids.

Gardner, H. (1983). *Frames of mind: The theory of multiple intelligences*. New York, NY: Basic Books.

Kagen, N. (Ed.). (1997). *What life was like in the age of chivalry: Medieval Europe, A.D. 800–1500*. Richmond, VA: Time-Life Books, Inc.

Jensen, E. (2001). *Arts with the brain in mind*. Alexandria, VA: Association for Supervision and Curriculum Development.

Liberty and Law (n.d.). *Economics for starters*. Retrieved April 28, 2007, from http://www.libertyandlaw.org/economicsfs.html.

McCarthy, B. (1990). Using the 4MAT system to bring learning styles to schools. *Educational Leadership, 48*(2), 31–37.

Mount, S. (2006, August). *Constitutional topic: Checks and balances*. Retrieved April 20, 2007, from the U.S. Constitution Online Web site: http://www.usconstitution.net/consttop_mlaw.html.

Mulder, H. (2006). *The Moors in Spain: How we almost lost our scientific roots (2000–2006)*. Retrieved May 23, 2007, from the Science and You Organization Web site: http://www.scienceandyou.org.

NASA: National Aeronautics and Space Administration. (n.d.). *Building a quadrant: NASA explorers 9–12 lesson*. Retrieved May 8, 2007, from http://www.nasaexplores.com/show_58_teacher_st.php?id=040427115956.

The National Archives. (n.d.). *New deal*. Retrieved May 22, 2007, from http://www.nara.gov.

National Council for the Social Studies. (2002). *Expectations of excellence: Curriculum standards for social studies*. Silver Spring, MD: National Council for the Social Studies (NCSS).

National Geographic. (n.d.). *Lewis and Clark timeline*. Retrieved March 23, 2007, from http://www.nationalgeographic.com/lewisandclark/resources_timeline_1806.html.

Oregon Trail Interpretive Center. (n.d.). *End of the Oregon Trail*. Retrieved May 15, 2007, from http://www.endoftheoregontrail.org/road2oregon/sa09chrono.html.

Ovey, F. M. (1995, May). *Muslim–Christian dialogue: Ecumenism, no. 116*. Retrieved May 16, 2007, from the Monastic Interreligious Dialogue Web site: http://www.monasticdialog.com/a.php?id=480 Muslim–Christian Dialogue.

Ronda, J. L. (1984). *Lewis and Clark among the Indians*. Lincoln, NE: University of Nebraska.

Scarre, C. (1993). *Smithsonian timelines of the ancient world*. New York, NY: Dorling Kindersley, Inc.

Schlesinger, M., Jr. (Ed.). (1933). *The almanac of American history* (Rev. ed.). Greenwich, CT: Barnes & Noble, Inc., Putnam Grosset Group.

Tate, M. L. (2003). *Worksheets don't grow dendrites: 20 instructional strategies that engage the brain*. Thousand Oaks, CA: Corwin Press.

Tierney, T. (1987). *American family of the Pilgrim period: Paper dolls in full color*. Mineola, NY: Dover Publishing.

United Nations Organization. (n.d.). Retrieved May 14, 2007, from http://www.un.org.

Wikimedia Foundation, Inc. (n.d.). *Dust bowl*. Retrieved May 25, 2007, from http://en.wikipedia.org/wiki/Dust_Bowl.

Wolfe, P. (2001). *Brain matters: Translating research into classroom practice*. Alexandria, VA: Association for Supervision and Curriculum Development.

Printed in the United States
By Bookmasters